BREAKING FREE
FROM THE
VICTIM
MENTALITY

TRANSFORM YOUR MINDSET TO EMBRACE COURAGE, RESILIENCE, AUTHENTICITY AND SELF-OWNERSHIP

DONOVAN GARETT

AlgoRhythms Studios, Ltd.

P.O. BOX 35643

Cleveland, Ohio 44135, U.S.A

DISCLAIMER. This publication is intended (but not guaranteed) to provide accurate information in regard to the subject matter covered. Some information may not be applicable to every reader or every situation. It is sold with the understanding that neither the author, publisher, nor any other person or entity connected with the creation, publication, or distribution of this publication provides legal, accounting, medical, or other professional services. If expert assistance is required, the services of a competent professional should be sought. Furthermore, this publication may contain business strategies, marketing methods, and other statements that, regardless of the experiences of some, may not produce the same results for you.

PRINT ISBN: 978-1-963267-14-3

E-BOOK ISBN: 978-1-963267-15-0

AUDIOBOOK ISBN: 978-1-963267-16-7

Library of Congress Control Number: 2024917356

Printed in the United States of America

Contents

Preface   V

1. Understanding the Victim Mentality   1

2. The Roots of Victim Mentality   17

3. How Media Reinforces the Victim Mentality   31

4. Challenging Limiting Beliefs   45

5. Taking Ownership of Your Life   59

6. The Journey to Empowerment   75

7. Overcoming Challenges, Setbacks and Failures   83

8. Embracing Change and Growth   97

9. Building Healthy Relationships   113

10. Practicing Gratitude, Mindfulness and Joy   135

11. Living an Empowered Life   147

12. A Few Final Thoughts   157

Where to Find Help   165

Preface
The Moment When I Lost It . . .

After pulling into the parking lot, I sat in my car crying uncontrollably for nearly 20 minutes before regaining the composure needed to walk into the office.

The year was 2013, and my life was an absolute mess. Having recently failed the Bar Exam, in debt up to my eyeballs, my job, my health, my marriage, and my mind were all in complete shambles.

It was the lowest point of my life.

But, at this exact moment, I started to gain clarity.

After pondering my plight for several weeks, I realized that I was the common denominator. I could no longer rely on the cycle of victimhood perpetuated by the events of my childhood, spun by the media, and discussed openly in the Black community. I couldn't blame *"the man"* (whoever that was) or society at large for my problems.

I had no choice but to accept accountability for my actions. The only person to blame was the face staring back at me in the mirror. I conceded that my life was the sum total of my decisions.

If I wanted my life to change, then I had to change.

Since then, I have been on a journey. I've used many of the strategies and tactics in this book to change my own mindset and focus on accountability and empowerment — not just for myself but for those around me.

The photo on the cover of this book is a fictitious representation of my continuous struggle and a constant reminder that my journey never ends.

Thank you for the opportunity to be a part of your journey too.

Donovan Garett

Chapter 1

Understanding the Victim Mentality

"Discontent, blaming, complaining, self-pity cannot serve as a foundation for a good future, no matter how much effort you make."

— Eckhart Tolle

T O BREAK FREE FROM a victim mentality, we must first understand what it is and how it may be impacting our lives. In this chapter, we'll define it, highlight its key characteristics, and discuss how it can subtly influence our thoughts, behaviors, and relationships.

Defining the Victim Mentality

Let's start by level-setting exactly what the victim mindset truly entails. A victim mentality is more than just a temporary reaction to difficult circumstances; it is a deeply ingrained way of thinking that can influence every aspect of a person's life.

In this section, we'll take a close look at the core characteristics of the victim mentality, distinguishing it from temporary feelings of victimhood that a person might experience during stressful situations. We'll also address common misconceptions about this mindset and clarify why it's not simply about blaming others or denying real struggles. Finally, we'll examine the psychological basis of the victim mentality, examining how this way of thinking keeps individuals stuck in a cycle of powerlessness.

What is a Victim Mentality?

A victim mentality is a pervasive psychological state where people view themselves as perpetual victims of circumstances beyond their control. This mindset is characterized by a consistent pattern of blaming external factors for one's problems, coupled with a belief that nothing can be done to alter them. It involves a deep-seated feeling of helplessness, which leads to a sense of resignation and passivity.

Unlike temporary victimhood, which occurs in response to specific events such as a loss or failure, a chronic victim mentality is not limited to one situation. Instead, it becomes a default way of thinking.

People with a victim mentality often feel that life is inherently unfair to them, and they may adopt a narrative where they are always on the receiving end of mistreatment or bad luck. This mindset can permeate relationships, work, and personal goals, creating a cycle that reinforces their negative view of the world.

In everyday scenarios, this might show up when someone repeatedly blames their lack of success to the actions of others. For example, they might say, *"I can't get ahead because my boss never gives me a chance,"* or *"Things never work out for me because other people always have it easier."* These statements reflect an external locus of control, where the individual believes that their fate is determined by outside forces rather than by their own choices and actions.

Common Misconceptions

One of the most common misconceptions about the victim mentality is that it's simply an excuse to avoid responsibility. While it's true that those with a victim mentality may deflect blame onto others, this behavior often stems from deep psychological patterns rather than a conscious choice to avoid responsibility. The victim mentality is not about inventing or exaggerating problems; the struggles faced are real. However, the issue lies in how these struggles are interpreted.

Another misconception is that the victim mentality is easily overcome by simply deciding to think differently. In reality, this mindset is deeply ingrained and reinforced by cognitive distortions and past experiences. It is not just a surface-level attitude but a fundamental way of viewing oneself and the world. People with a victim mentality genuinely believe that they are powerless to change their circumstances, which makes breaking free from this mindset a complex process that requires more than just positive thinking.

It's also important to understand that having a victim mentality does not invalidate or lessen the actual pain or injustice someone has experienced. However, the critical difference lies in how the person moves forward. Someone with a victim mentality often becomes stuck in a cycle of focusing on the wrongs they've endured rather than seeking ways to heal, grow, or move past their situation. Recognizing that this mindset is a psychological construct rather than an objective reality is vital for making meaningful changes.

Psychological Factors

The victim mentality is deeply rooted in several psychological factors, many of which involve cognitive distortions. Cognitive distortions are irrational or exaggerated thought patterns that negatively influence perception and behavior. One of the most common distortions seen in the victim mentality is *"all-or-nothing"* thinking.

This type of thinking causes individuals to see situations in black-and-white terms without acknowledging the nuances or complexities of life. For example, if someone fails at a task, they may think, *"I'm a complete failure,"* instead of recognizing that failure in one area does not define their entire worth or potential.

Another cognitive distortion is overgeneralization, where a person takes a single negative event and applies it broadly to unrelated aspects of their life. For instance, if they experience a rejection in one context, they might conclude, *"I'm always rejected,"* or *"Nothing ever goes right for me,"* even when these beliefs are not objectively valid. This creates a mental environment where the individual constantly expects and perceives negative outcomes, which, in turn, reinforces their sense of victimhood.

The psychological basis of the victim mentality also involves learned helplessness, which occurs when an individual believes they have no control over a situation, even when they do. Over time, this belief becomes generalized to other areas of life, leading to a persistent sense of powerlessness.

For instance, I occasionally overhear people saying things like, *"There are no good jobs out there"* or *"All the good men are already taken."* The person making this statement fails to realize that these beliefs are self-reinforcing because the more a person believes they are helpless, the less likely they are to take action to change their circumstances, which, in time, validates their original belief.

Understanding these psychological underpinnings is key to recognizing the patterns of thought and behavior that contribute to the victim mentality. By identifying and addressing these cognitive distortions, individuals can challenge their assumptions and take the first steps toward reclaiming control over their lives.

Recognizing Signs and Symptoms

Understanding the victim mentality is only the first step; recognizing its presence in our own lives is where *real* change begins.

Let's explore the emotional and behavioral patterns often accompanying a victim mentality, helping you identify whether these tendencies might be affecting you. We'll also examine how self-sabotaging thoughts can perpetuate this mindset, keeping you trapped in a cycle of negativity. Finally, we'll analyze the role of language and communication in reinforcing a victim mentality, highlighting how your words and expressions might be contributing to a sense of powerlessness.

Emotional and Behavioral Patterns

The victim mentality often manifests itself through distinct emotional and behavioral patterns that can be observed in daily interactions. Emotionally, individuals frequently experience feelings of helplessness, which, if not addressed, often leads to hopelessness, where they feel that no matter what they do, nothing will ever improve. Over time, these emotions can solidify into chronic resentment as they perceive themselves as unfairly treated by life, others, or even fate.

Behaviorally, the victim mentality often reveals itself through passive-aggressiveness, where individuals express their anger or frustration indirectly rather than confronting issues head-on.

Another common sign is blame-shifting, where responsibility for mistakes or failures is consistently placed on others or external factors. This is often accompanied by avoidance of responsibility, where the person refuses to acknowledge their role in their own challenges, preferring instead to see themselves as a powerless observer of their own life.

Self-Sabotaging Thoughts

Negative self-talk is a hallmark of the victim mentality and perpetuates the cycle of defeat and disempowerment. Individuals with this mindset frequently engage in self-sabotaging thoughts that undermine their confidence and ability to take positive action.

These thoughts often take the form of questions or statements that reinforce a sense of inadequacy or victimhood, such as *"Why does this always happen to me?"* or *"I can't do anything right."* These are not merely passing doubts; they become ingrained beliefs that shape a person's self-perception and behavior.

Another common self-sabotaging thought is the belief that nothing is their fault. This belief absolves the person of responsibility for their actions or circumstances, making it easier to maintain the victim mentality. These thoughts are self-reinforcing: the more a person believes them, the more they act in ways that validate these beliefs, creating a cycle that is difficult to break.

The Role of Language and Communication

Language also plays a crucial role in reflecting a victim mentality. How a person speaks about their experiences can reveal much about their mindset. For instance, phrases like *"They made me feel..."* suggest that the speaker believes their emotions are entirely controlled by others rather than by their own interpretations or reactions.

Similarly, the expression *"I have no choice..."* indicates a belief in powerlessness, where the individual feels trapped by circumstances beyond their control. These patterns of communication not only reveal a victim mentality but also reinforce it, as the language that a person uses shapes and solidifies their beliefs and attitudes.

By consistently framing experiences in terms of helplessness and lack of control, people strengthen their identification with the victim role, making it harder to adopt a more empowered mindset. Recognizing and changing these language patterns is a crucial step in breaking free from the victim mentality and reclaiming personal power.

Impact on Personal Growth

A victim mentality doesn't just affect how you see yourself; it has far-reaching consequences for your personal growth and the quality of your relationships. Here, we'll look at how this mindset can lead to stagnation, holding you back from achieving your potential in both your personal and professional life. We'll also explore the strain it can place on your relationships, often leading to conflict, codependency, and isolation. Lastly, we'll discuss how a victim mentality creates a self-perpetuating cycle of negativity that undermines your mental health, self-worth, and overall life satisfaction.

Stagnation and Lack of Personal Growth

A victim mentality significantly hampers personal and professional growth by promoting a mindset that is resistant to change and self-improvement. Individuals trapped in this mindset often struggle to advance in their careers or personal lives because they view obstacles as insurmountable and external forces as the sole determinants of their success or failure. This perspective leads to stagnation, where the person remains stuck in the same behaviors, unable to move forward or achieve their goals.

There is a strong connection between victim mentality and procrastination. When individuals believe that their efforts will ultimately be futile, they are more likely to delay taking action or avoid it altogether. A deep-seated fear of failure often drives this procrastination; rather than risk failure by trying, a person may choose inaction to protect themselves from potential disappointment. Over time, this behavior erodes self-esteem as they internalize their lack of progress as a reflection of their inherent worth or abilities, further entrenching the victim mentality.

Strained Relationships

The victim mentality also takes a heavy toll on relationships, whether with family, friends, or romantic partners. Individuals with this mentality often engage in behaviors that strain these connections, such as constant complaining, blame-shifting, or refusing to take responsibility for their role in conflicts. These behaviors create tension and frustration in relationships, as others may feel burdened by the person's negativity and lack of accountability.

Victim mentality can also lead to codependency, where one person's need to play the role of the victim is matched by another's need to play the role of the rescuer. This dynamic can create unhealthy relationships where both parties are stuck in roles that limit personal growth and mutual respect.

Additionally, the constant focus on perceived injustices or wrongs can lead to frequent conflict, as the individual with a victim mentality may react defensively or aggressively to any perceived criticism. Over time, these patterns can result in isolation, as others may distance themselves to avoid the negativity and drama accompanying the relationship.

The Cycle of Victimhood

One of the most insidious aspects of a victim mentality is that it creates a self-perpetuating cycle of negativity. When individuals consistently view themselves as victims, they are more likely to see new experiences through this lens, reinforcing their belief that they are powerless to change their circumstances. This belief affects their present actions and shapes their future as they continue to make choices based on the belief that they are destined to fail or be mistreated.

The long-term effects of this cycle can be devastating to a person's mental health. Chronic feelings of helplessness and hopelessness can lead to depression, anxiety, and other mental health issues.

Moreover, the constant focus on what is wrong, rather than what can be changed or improved, erodes self-worth, leaving the individual with a diminished sense of identity and purpose. Over time, this can result in a profound dissatisfaction with life, as the person feels trapped in a narrative where they are always the victim but never the hero of their own story.

Victim Mentality and Entitlement

The relationship between a victim mentality and a sense of entitlement is complex and deeply intertwined. While on the surface, these two mindsets might seem contradictory—one rooted in powerlessness and the other in an expectation of unearned privileges—they often coexist, feeding into and reinforcing each other in subtle but significant ways.

Entitlement Through the Lens of a Victim Mentality

Entitlement is the belief that one deserves certain privileges, treatment, or outcomes without necessarily having to earn them through effort or merit. When paired with a victim mentality, entitlement manifests as an expectation that others (or the world) should compensate a person for perceived injustices or hardships.

> **TIP:** The next time you watch the news, take a closer look at some of the so-called *"social justice"* movements. Can you identify common themes of victimization and entitlement?

For instance, an individual with a victim mentality may feel that because they have suffered or been wronged, they are owed something in return—whether that be special treatment, opportunities, or the avoidance of consequences or penalties for their actions. This entitlement can stem from a deep-seated belief that life has been unfair to them and, therefore, they deserve more than others as a form of compensation.

The Reinforcing Cycle of Victimhood and Entitlement

The interplay between victim mentality and entitlement creates a reinforcing cycle that can be difficult to break. Here's how it typically works:

1. *Perceived Injustice or Hardship:* The individual experiences a setback or perceives that they have been treated unfairly. This strengthens the victim mentality, where they see themselves as powerless and at the mercy of external forces.

2. *Sense of Entitlement:* As a response to this perceived injustice, the individual develops a sense of entitlement, believing that they are owed something in return. This might include expecting others to fix their problems, give them special treatment, or absolve them of responsibility.

3. *Disappointment and Resentment:* When the world does not meet these expectations—when others do not provide the expected compensation or special treatment—the individual feels further victimized. This disappointment reinforces their original belief that they are a victim, deepening both the victim mentality and the sense of entitlement.

4. *Avoidance of Responsibility:* The sense of entitle-

ment often leads to avoiding personal responsibility. The individual may feel that since they are owed something, they should not have to put in the effort to change their circumstances. This further entrenches the victim mentality, as their lack of action perpetuates the cycle of powerlessness and dissatisfaction.

The Consequences of This Interplay

The combination of victim mentality and entitlement can have far-reaching consequences in various areas of life:

Relationships: Entitlement strains relationships, as the person might place unrealistic demands on other people (or even the government), expecting them to fulfill needs or desires they feel entitled to due to their perceived victimhood. This can lead to resentment on both sides and erode trust and mutual respect in relationships.

Personal Growth: The belief that one is entitled to success, happiness, or other outcomes without effort stifles personal growth. When individuals expect rewards without taking responsibility or doing the necessary work, they are less likely to engage in behaviors that lead to genuine progress and achievement.

Mental Health: The interplay between victim mentality and entitlement can exacerbate feelings of frustration, anger, and helplessness. When the world does not meet their expectations, the individual may spiral deeper into negativity, which can contribute to depression, anxiety, and a persistent sense of dissatisfaction with life.

In the next chapter, we'll dig deeper and explore the roots of victim mentality, emphasizing the influence of childhood experiences, cultural and societal factors, and trauma.

Chapter 2
The Roots of Victim Mentality

"The paradox of trauma is that it has both the power
to destroy and the power to transform and resurrect."
— Peter A. Levine

U NDERSTANDING THE ORIGINS OF a victim mentality is key to overcoming it. In this chapter, we discuss the deep-seated origins of this mindset, looking at how childhood experiences, cultural and societal influences, and trauma shape the way we see ourselves and the world. By uncovering these roots, you'll be better equipped to recognize factors that may have contributed to your own victim mentality and begin the process of shifting to a more empowered way of thinking.

Childhood Experiences

Our earliest experiences play a pivotal role in shaping who we become, and this is especially true when it comes to the development of a victim mentality. In this section, we'll explore how childhood conditioning and learned behaviors from parents, caregivers, and authority figures can set the stage for a mindset of powerlessness. We'll also examine the influence of attachment styles on how we perceive ourselves and our ability to navigate life's challenges. Finally, we'll see how childhood trauma can profoundly impact self-perception and foster a deep-seated sense of helplessness that often carries into adulthood.

Early Conditioning and Learned Behavior

Foundational beliefs and behaviors are formed during childhood, many of which persist into adulthood. During these formative years, children absorb messages from their environment that shape their self-concept, view of the world, and expectations of life. The beliefs children develop about themselves and the world are heavily influenced by the behaviors and attitudes modeled by parents, caregivers, and authority figures.

If a child frequently witnesses a parent blaming external factors for their problems, they may internalize this behavior as normal, leading them to adopt a similar mindset. Conversely, if a child sees caregivers taking responsibility for their actions and working to overcome challenges, they are more likely to develop an empowered outlook. These early lessons in accountability, or the lack thereof, set the stage for whether a child grows up with a victim mentality or a mindset of personal responsibility.

Children also internalize subtle messages about their worth and capabilities based on how they are treated and what is expected of them. A child who is consistently told that they are helpless or incapable may grow up believing these things to be true, which can lead to a victim mentality. On the other hand, a child who is encouraged to try new things, take risks, and learn from failures is more likely to develop a resilient, empowered mindset.

The Role of Attachment Styles

Attachment styles, which are formed in early childhood based on interactions with primary caregivers, play a significant role in shaping an individual's mindset and approach to relationships. Attachment styles, including secure, anxious, and avoidant, influence how a person perceives themselves and others.

A secure attachment style develops when a child's needs are consistently met with care and attention. This typically leads to a healthy sense of self-worth and trust in others. These individuals are more likely to approach life confidently and believe in their ability to influence outcomes.

In contrast, an anxious attachment style, characterized by inconsistent or unpredictable care, can breed a sense of helplessness and dependency. Individuals with this attachment style may grow up feeling insecure and unsure of their ability to manage life's challenges. They often look to others for validation and support in ways that perpetuate a victim mentality.

Similarly, an avoidant attachment style, arising from emotionally distant or unresponsive caregivers, can lead to a mindset where the person feels they must fend for themselves but also believes that their efforts will not make a difference. This combination of independence and resignation can contribute to a sense of powerlessness, reinforcing the victim mentality.

There is also a connection between early attachment experiences and adult relationships. Individuals with insecure attachment styles may struggle with trust, intimacy, and self-esteem, all of which can contribute to a victim mentality in adulthood. Understanding and addressing these early attachment issues is a crucial step in breaking free from a victim mindset.

Childhood Trauma and Victim Mentality

Childhood trauma has a lasting impact on an individual's self-perception and view of society, often laying the groundwork for a victim mentality in adulthood. Trauma can take many forms, including physical, emotional, or sexual abuse, neglect, or witnessing violence. These experiences can fundamentally alter how a child sees themselves and their place in the world.

When a child experiences trauma, especially without subsequent support and healing, they may come to see themselves as inherently flawed, unworthy, or powerless. This distorted self-image can persist into adulthood, leading to a chronic sense of victimhood. The belief that they are undeserving of happiness or incapable of escaping their past can easily trap individuals in a cycle of negative thinking and self-sabotaging behaviors.

If you or someone you know needs mental health support, a list of FREE resources in the U.S., Canada, U.K. and Mexico is provided at the end of this book. See the section *"Where to Find Help"*.

Unresolved trauma often manifests in adulthood as a victim mentality because the individual continues to operate from the belief that their past experiences define them. This can lead to feelings of helplessness, where the person believes that no matter what they do, they will never be able to overcome the damage done to them. This mindset not only affects personal growth but also relationships, career, and overall quality of life.

Trauma can also distort how individuals perceive others and the world around them. They may become hypervigilant, expecting harm or betrayal in every interaction, reinforcing their sense of perpetual victimhood. Breaking free from this mindset requires acknowledging the trauma, understanding its impact on their life, and working through it with the help of professional therapy that focuses on healing and empowerment.

Cultural and Societal Factors

Our environment significantly shapes our beliefs and attitudes, often in ways we may not immediately recognize. In this section, we'll see how societal messages and cultural conditioning can reinforce a victim mentality, subtly influencing how we see ourselves and our place in the world. We'll also discuss the impact of systemic oppression and marginalization, examining how these external factors can contribute to a mindset of helplessness. Finally, we'll discuss the power of collective beliefs within communities and how these shared narratives can either trap individuals in a cycle of victimhood or, conversely, help them break free.

Societal Messaging

Societal norms play a powerful role in shaping individual mindsets, often reinforcing the victim mentality through subtle and overt messages. From a young age, we are exposed to cultural narratives that define what is possible or acceptable based on our gender, race, socioeconomic status, and other identifiers. These narratives often promote stereotypes and expectations that subconsciously confine us to specific roles (commonly aligning with societal expectations), further limiting personal empowerment.

Societal expectations also play a significant role in reinforcing a victim mentality. When society imposes stringent expectations based on factors like gender, ethnicity, or class, individuals may feel trapped by these roles, believing they have no choice but to conform. This can foster resentment and a belief that they are victims of a system they cannot change. Challenging these societal norms and reclaiming personal agency is crucial for breaking free from a victim mentality.

Marginalization and Oppression

Systemic oppression and marginalization also have a profound impact on mindset, often contributing to a victim mentality. People who experience discrimination, exclusion, or economic hardship due to their race, gender, sexual orientation, or other aspects of their identity may come to see the world as inherently hostile or unjust. This can lead to a deep-seated belief that they are powerless to change their circumstances, reinforcing feelings of victimhood.

It is important to recognize that marginalization experiences are real and can create significant barriers to success and well-being. However, there is a distinction between acknowledging these external barriers and internalizing them as a defining characteristic of one's identity. When individuals internalize oppression, they may adopt a mindset where they see themselves as permanently disadvantaged, unable to rise above the challenges they face.

This internalization of victimhood is particularly harmful, as it commonly prevents people from recognizing their own agency and potential for change. While systemic issues must be addressed at a societal level, it is equally important to realize that these external forces do not solely define us. Empowerment begins with the belief that, despite barriers, an individual can still take meaningful steps to improve their life.

The Power of Collective Beliefs

Collective beliefs and shared experiences within communities can significantly influence individual mindsets, often reinforcing a victim mentality. When a group shares a history of oppression or marginalization, a collective narrative may develop, emphasizing collective victimhood rather than supportive empowerment. While rooted in real experiences, these narratives often limit the ability to see beyond shared struggles and focus on the possibilities for growth.

The power of group identity is strong, and individuals commonly align their personal beliefs with those of the community to which they belong, even when those beliefs limit their potential for growth.

Breaking free from collective victimhood narratives is possible. It requires a person to recognize the influence of these collective beliefs and to challenge the notion that the struggles of the community define their identity. By cultivating a sense of empowerment within the context of a supportive community, a person can shift the narrative from one of victimhood to one of resilience.

Strategies for breaking free from collective victimhood include seeking out positive role models who have overcome similar challenges, engaging in community discussions that focus on empowerment rather than victimization, and encouraging a mindset of growth and possibility.

Trauma's Role in Shaping Mindset

Trauma leaves deep imprints on the mind, profoundly affecting how we perceive ourselves and the world around us. In this section, we'll take a look at the psychological impact of trauma, focusing on how it can lead to feelings of helplessness, fear, and disempowerment that are central to the victim mentality. We'll also see how trauma-induced cognitive distortions can warp thinking patterns, reinforcing a negative self-view and a sense of powerlessness. Finally, we'll discuss the importance of healing from trauma to break free from these destructive patterns and foster a mindset of resilience and empowerment.

The Psychology of Trauma

Trauma has a profound impact on the brain and can significantly alter how we perceive and interact with the world. When a person experiences trauma, the brain's natural response is to enter a state of heightened alertness, often referred to as the *"fight, flight, or freeze"* response. This is designed to protect us from immediate harm but can lead to long-lasting changes in how our brains process information and emotions.

Trauma commonly leaves people with feelings of helplessness, fear, and disempowerment. These emotions stem from the overwhelming nature of the traumatic event, which makes the individual feel as though they have no control over the situation. As a result, they may begin to view themselves as perpetual victims, unable to influence the outcome of their lives. This mindset can persist long after the traumatic event has passed, shaping how they respond to new challenges and stressors.

Post-traumatic stress responses, such as hypervigilance, intrusive thoughts, and emotional numbness, further reinforce this mindset. These responses are the brain's way of shielding the individual from future harm but can lead to a cycle of negative thinking and avoidance behaviors. Understanding these patterns is crucial for recognizing the role trauma plays in shaping a victim mentality.

Trauma-Induced Cognitive Distortions

Trauma can lead to cognitive distortions, which are irrational or exaggerated thought patterns that negatively influence how individuals perceive themselves and the world around them. One common distortion is catastrophizing, where the individual expects the worst possible outcome in any situation. This thinking pattern is often rooted in the fear and helplessness experienced during the traumatic event and can lead to a persistent sense of doom and powerlessness.

Another common cognitive distortion linked to trauma is over-generalization. This occurs when an individual takes a single negative experience and applies it broadly to unrelated areas of their life. For example, if someone was betrayed by a close friend, they might begin to believe that all people are untrustworthy. This type of thinking reinforces the victim mentality by making the individual feel as though they are constantly under threat, even in situations where no real danger exists.

These cognitive distortions are powerful because they shape how individuals interpret their experiences. When left unchecked, they can create a *"self-fulfilling prophecy,"* where a person's negative expectations influence their actions and lead to the very outcomes they fear. Recognizing these distortions and learning to challenge them is a critical step in breaking free from the victim mentality.

Techniques for identifying and challenging trauma-induced cognitive distortions include mindfulness practices, cognitive-behavioral therapy (CBT)[1], and journaling. By becoming aware of these distorted thoughts and questioning their validity, a person can begin to reframe their experiences and develop a more balanced and empowered perspective.

---

1. See, e.g., Choosing Therapy, *Trauma-Focused CBT (TF-CBT): How It Works, Examples, & Effectiveness*, https://www.choosingtherapy.com/trauma-focused-cbt/and N.I.M.H., *Evaluation of cognitive restructuring for post-traumatic stress disorder in people with severe mental illness*, https://www.ncbi.nlm.nih.gov/pmc/articles/PMC4450219/

Healing Trauma to Overcome Victim Mentality

Healing from trauma is essential for shifting from a victim mentality to a mindset of empowerment. Unresolved trauma keeps individuals locked in patterns of fear, helplessness, and negative thinking, making it difficult to move forward. Addressing the underlying trauma allows individuals to process their experiences, release the hold these events have on their lives, and rebuild their self-image.

There are various therapeutic approaches that can help people heal from trauma and reframe their experiences. Cognitive-behavioral therapy (CBT) is one effective method, as it focuses on identifying and changing negative thought patterns. Eye Movement Desensitization and Reprocessing (EMDR) is another therapy[2] that has shown success in helping individuals process traumatic memories and reduce their emotional impact. Other approaches, such as somatic therapy[3], focus on releasing trauma stored in the body, helping individuals reconnect with

---

2. See, e.g., The Cleveland Clinic, *EMDR Therapy*, https://my.clevelandclinic.org/health/treatments/22641-emdr-therapy and The American Psychological Association, *Eye Movement Desensitization and Reprocessing (EMDR) Therapy*, https://www.apa.org/ptsd-guideline/treatments/eye-movement-reprocessing

3. See, e.g., Harvard Medical School, *What is somatic therapy?*, https://www.health.harvard.edu/blog/what-is-somatic-therapy-202307072951

their physical selves, and reducing symptoms of post-traumatic stress.

In addition to formal therapy, self-compassion and patience are crucial elements of the healing process. Trauma recovery is not linear, and setbacks will occur along the way. Victims of trauma need to treat themselves with kindness and understanding, recognizing that healing takes time. By cultivating self-compassion, they can rebuild their sense of self-worth and develop a more empowered outlook on life.

Ultimately, healing trauma is about reclaiming power and agency. It involves acknowledging the pain of the past but refusing to let it dictate the future. By working through trauma and challenging the associated cognitive distortions, individuals can break free from the victim mentality and start living a life defined by resilience, strength, and empowerment.

In the next chapter, we'll examine the role of media, social media, entertainment, and pop culture in reinforcing the victim mentality.

Chapter 3

How Media Reinforces the Victim Mentality

"Almost everything will work again if you unplug it for a few minutes, including you."
— Anne Lamott

I N ADDITION TO THE messaging and social conditioning we receive from a very young age, the media, social media, entertainment, and pop culture greatly influence our perceptions and beliefs. The narratives they promote often shape how we see ourselves and others. While these platforms offer valuable information and connections, they can also amplify feelings of helplessness that reinforce a victim mentality.

Constant exposure to sensational news, curated social media feeds, and disempowering storylines in entertainment subtly guide people into a mindset where they view challenges as beyond their control. This is done through the use of both overt and covert messaging carefully embedded into the storylines of movies, TV shows, and other media. The repetition of victim-centered content makes it easier to internalize this outlook, leaving people feeling powerless in their own lives. This chapter explores how various forms of media contribute to these feelings. By understanding the effects of media on mindset and behavior, we can make better choices about the content we consume.

The Influence of Media and Pop Culture

Media and pop culture are powerful forces that shape our thoughts, behaviors, and beliefs. Television, films, news outlets, social media, and music constantly expose us to messages that influence how we view ourselves and the world around us. These pervasive influences often affect us in ways we may not fully recognize.

In this section, we look at how media and pop culture can reinforce a victim mentality by consistently presenting narratives that focus on helplessness, fear, and conflict. By understanding how these platforms shape our perceptions, we can begin to recognize their impact on our mindset. This awareness is the first step toward making conscious choices about the content we engage with.

How Media Shapes Our Perceptions

Media plays an undeniably powerful role in shaping public perceptions and influencing societal norms. Through traditional news outlets, social media platforms, and entertainment channels, we are constantly shown narratives that impact how we see the world and how we interact with it. The stories that are highlighted, the headlines that grab our attention, and the content we engage with all contribute to our understanding of reality (whether accurate or not). Media serves as a lens, guiding us on what to focus on, what to care about, and how to interpret the events unfolding around us.

The media is incredibly influential as a tool for narrative building. Through selective reporting, story framing, and repetition of certain themes, the media constructs narratives that resonate widely, shaping public opinion and collective behavior. Whether through the news we watch, the social media posts we scroll through, or the movies and TV shows we enjoy, these narratives often reflect and reinforce cultural norms, including those related to power dynamics and victimhood.

TIP: If you doubt the power of media to shape perceptions, examine history. Some of the richest, most powerful people in history were (and still are) the owners of vast media empires.

However, the media does much more than just mirror society; it actively shapes societal attitudes. When perspectives such as the victim mentality are consistently emphasized, they become ingrained in the collective consciousness. This continuous exposure can normalize these attitudes, making them more entrenched and difficult to challenge. Recognizing this is paramount to understanding how media can reflect and solidify societal beliefs that may not serve our best interests.

Pop Culture's Impact on Self-Identity

Pop culture, which includes movies, television, music, and celebrity culture, significantly shapes individual identities and self-perceptions. The characters we admire, the music that resonates with us, and the celebrities we follow all play a role in constructing our self-image. Pop culture offers models of behavior, success, and even victimhood, which can heavily influence how we define ourselves and our roles in society.

Victimhood is a recurring theme in pop culture. Whether in films, television shows, or music, the portrayal of victim-based stereotypes can subtly reinforce the idea that being a victim is a dominant or inevitable aspect of life. When these portrayals are glorified or presented as the standard response to adversity, they can shape viewers' mindsets, leading them to internalize victimhood as a central part of their identity.

Moreover, pop culture often perpetuates stereotypes that contribute to a sense of learned helplessness or victimhood. These stereotypes, which are often based on factors such as gender, race, or socio-economic status, often depict certain groups as inherently reliant on others for support or powerless. This re-inforcement of self-limiting stories can restrict how individuals view themselves and their potential, feeding them a narrative that focuses on limitations rather than possibilities.

Media Consumption and Mental Health

The content we consume through media has a profound impact on our mental health. When we are exposed to a constant stream of negative or victim-centered media, it can lead to feelings of anxiety, depression, and a reduced sense of control over our lives. The continuous bombardment of images and stories that emphasize suffering and helplessness can wear down our psychological resilience, making it harder to maintain a positive and empowered outlook on life.

News Media and the Victim Mentality

The news media wields significant power in shaping public consciousness. Every day, millions of people turn to news outlets to understand the events that unfold in the world around them. However, the way these stories are presented often goes beyond mere reporting. The narratives constructed by news media can heavily influence how we perceive ourselves, our communities, and our place in society.

In this section, we will discuss how the news media reinforces the victim mentality. Through sensationalism, the focus on fear-based narratives, and commonly framing stories in terms of conflict and division, the news often amplifies feelings of helplessness and powerlessness. By understanding these methods, we can better recognize when we are being influenced and take steps to maintain a more balanced and empowered view of the world.

Sensationalism and the Culture of Fear

Sensationalist reporting has become a staple of modern news media, where the focus on dramatic and fear-based narratives often dominates headlines. This approach to news isn't just designed to grab attention but also to influence how we perceive the world around us. News stories constantly framed around crisis, conflict, and catastrophe promote a sense of helplessness and victimization among viewers. The emphasis on fear can distort our worldview, making it seem as though danger and disaster are ever-present and inevitable.

The psychological impact of constant exposure to negative news cannot be overstated. When we are bombarded with stories that highlight the worst aspects of humanity and the world, it can lead to increased anxiety, stress, and a diminished sense of agency. Over time, this exposure can contribute to a victim mentality, where individuals begin to see themselves as powerless in the face of overwhelming external forces. Understanding the role of sensationalism in shaping our perceptions is crucial for maintaining mental health.

TIP: If you watch the news on TV, stop for three days. See if feelings of anxiety, depression, and frustration begin to subside. If something truly earth-shattering occurs, you'll know about it (phone alerts, family, friends, etc.).

The Perpetuation of "Us vs. Them" Narratives

The news media frequently frames stories in terms of conflict and division, creating an *"us vs. them"* dynamic that reinforces a victim-villain narrative. This binary approach oversimplifies complex issues, reducing them to a battle between opposing sides. In doing so, the media assigns specific groups as perpetual victims while others are cast as oppressors or villains. This type of reporting entrenches feelings of victimhood by constantly emphasizing division and conflict, rather than cooperation or mutual understanding.

This thinking pattern profoundly affects both social cohesion and individual self-perception. When people are repeatedly exposed to narratives that highlight division, it can lead to polarization, where individuals see themselves and others through a lens of opposition rather than humanity. This polarization affects social relationships and reinforces a sense of powerlessness as they feel trapped in a larger struggle beyond their control.

The Role of Media Bias in Shaping Victim Narratives

Media bias, whether political, cultural, or ideological, also shapes how stories are framed and certain groups are portrayed. Biased reporting can influence public perception, often reinforcing victim identities. When media outlets present stories with a particular slant, they can shape the narrative to position certain groups as victims, heightening a sense of powerlessness and dependency.

The consequences of biased reporting are far-reaching. It not only skews public understanding of complex issues but also contributes to the entrenchment of victim identities within specific communities. This can perpetuate cycles of dependency and helplessness, making it harder for individuals to break free from the narratives imposed upon them.

To combat the victim mentality, it is essential to engage critically with news. This means being aware of potential biases, seeking out diverse sources of information, and always questioning the narratives presented. By doing so, you can protect yourself from the influence of biased reporting and consume media with a more balanced perspective.

Social Media's Amplification of Victimhood

Social media platforms offer unprecedented opportunities for connection and expression but also have significant downsides. One of the most concerning aspects of social media is its ability to amplify negative narratives, including those that reinforce a victim mentality.

In this section, we'll take a look at how social media platforms contribute to the amplification of victimhood. From the way algorithms prioritize content to the creation of echo chambers, the highly addictive nature of social media can trap users in cycles of negativity and helplessness. The constant exposure to curated, often extreme content can shape how individuals see themselves and the world around them, reinforcing feelings of powerlessness and entrenching a victim mindset.

We will also examine the impact of online communities and influencers who, intentionally or not, promote victimhood as part of their identity or brand. By understanding these dynamics, we can better navigate social media in a way that supports empowerment rather than diminishes it. Recognizing the power of social media to shape our thoughts and behaviors is the first step in using these platforms more mindfully and positively.

"There is a valid reason social media is linked to depression and loneliness. We live in a time when many people spend countless hours a day online strolling through the timeline of others with envy, regret, and little appreciation for their own life."

— Germany Kent

The "Echo Chamber" Effect of Social Media

Social media algorithms are designed to keep users engaged by showing them content that aligns with their existing beliefs and preferences. This creates echo chambers—environments where users are repeatedly exposed to the same ideas and narratives. For those who already lean toward a victim mentality, this can mean a constant reinforcement of victim narratives, making it difficult to see beyond these perspectives.

The psychological impact of echo chambers can be profound. When individuals are consistently exposed to content emphasizing helplessness and victimization, these feelings feel like an inescapable part of reality. The more a person engages with this content, the more entrenched these beliefs become, leading to a cycle of negativity that is hard to break.

To counteract this effect, it's crucial to vary social media consumption. By intentionally viewing content that challenges existing beliefs and presents different perspectives, users can broaden their understanding and develop a more balanced view of the world. This approach helps break the constant cycle of consuming victim-based content and promotes a more resilient mindset.

Social Media, Comparison, and Envy

Social media platforms are designed to showcase the best of people's lives, creating an environment for unhealthy comparisons. When users constantly compare their lives to the idealized images they see online, it often leads to feelings of inadequacy and victimhood. The perception that others are living better, more fulfilling lives can deepen feelings of being unfairly treated or left behind.

Influencers play a significant role in this dynamic. They often present a polished, curated version of reality that sets unrealistic standards for success, beauty, and happiness. This can negatively impact self-esteem, leading their audience to internalize a sense of failure or victimhood when their lives do not measure up to these idealized images.

It's important to practice mindful social media use to counteract these effects. This includes being aware of the curated nature of online content and recognizing that what is presented is not always an accurate reflection of reality. Users can protect their mental health and cultivate a more positive self-image by consciously limiting exposure to content that triggers negative comparisons and focusing on content that truly educates, inspires, and uplifts.

Escapism and Passive Consumption

Entertainment often serves as a form of escapism, allowing viewers to step away from the realities of their own lives momentarily. While this can be a healthy way to relax, it can also lead to passive consumption of media that reinforces victim narratives. When individuals passively consume content that centers around victimhood without critically engaging with it, they risk internalizing these disempowering messages.

This passive consumption can subtly shape viewers' mindsets, reinforcing the idea that they are victims of circumstances beyond their control. Over time, this can erode resilience and diminish the drive to take proactive steps in their own lives. By being mindful of the messages we consume and seeking out narratives that inspire and uplift, we can use entertainment as a tool for entertainment rather than a trap that reinforces disempowerment.

Why It's Important to Develop Critical Media Literacy

Developing critical media literacy is essential at a time when we are constantly bombarded with information. Critical media literacy involves analyzing and evaluating the content we consume. Instead of passively accepting media messages, it's important to approach content with a questioning mindset. Ask yourself who created the content, what their intentions might be, and how it might be influencing your thoughts and beliefs.

By questioning the media you engage with, you can uncover the subtle ways it may be shaping your perception of yourself and the world. Understanding the influence media has on behavior and mindset is a powerful tool for empowerment. It allows you to take control of your media consumption, ensuring that it supports your growth rather than undermining it. Developing these skills enables you to filter out content that does not serve your best interests.

Curating a Balanced Media Diet

Just as a healthy diet requires balance, so does your media consumption. Curating a balanced media diet involves intentionally selecting content that inspires, educates, and empowers you. This doesn't mean avoiding all negative news or controversial topics but rather ensuring that your media intake includes a variety of perspectives and a healthy dose of positive, uplifting content.

Reducing exposure to negative media, such as sensationalist news or disempowering entertainment, can significantly improve your mindset and outlook on life. Diversifying your sources of information also helps to break out of echo chambers, exposing you to a wider range of ideas and encouraging a more well-rounded perspective.

In our next chapter, we'll examine strategies for combating the victim mentality. We'll start with a structured approach to challenging limiting beliefs, cultivating self-awareness, and understanding the power of perspective. These elements are crucial for breaking free from the victim mentality and nurturing a mindset of empowerment.

Chapter 4
Challenging Limiting Beliefs

"Remember, we see the world not as it is but as we are.
Most of us see through the eyes of our fears and our
limiting beliefs and our false assumptions."
— Robin S. Sharma

NOW THAT WE'VE SEEN the sources of the victim mentality, it's time to start dismantling the beliefs that limit our mindset and keep us trapped in a cycle of victim-based thinking, starting with limiting beliefs.

Limiting beliefs are powerful barriers that keep us trapped in a victim mentality, preventing us from realizing our full potential. In this chapter, we identify the self-defeating thoughts that hold you back and the importance of cultivating self-awareness. By challenging these limiting beliefs and shifting your perspective, you can begin to replace them with more empowering thoughts that support growth and positive change.

Identifying and Questioning Self-Defeating Thoughts

Our thoughts have a powerful influence on how we experience life, and when those thoughts are negative or self-defeating, they can keep us trapped in a cycle of victimhood. In this section, we'll focus on recognizing the self-defeating thoughts that often drive the victim mentality. We'll explore common patterns of negative thinking that undermine confidence and reinforce a sense of helplessness. Most importantly, we'll discuss strategies for questioning and challenging these thoughts, empowering you to replace them with more constructive and empowering beliefs.

What Are Limiting Beliefs?

Limiting beliefs are deeply ingrained thoughts that restrict your potential by convincing you that certain things are impossible or unattainable. These beliefs often form during childhood and are reinforced over time through repeated experiences and societal conditioning.

For example, a child who consistently hears messages that they are not smart enough or capable enough might grow up believing these things to be true, even in the face of evidence to the contrary. Once established, limiting beliefs become mental filters through which you view the world, affecting every decision you make.

These beliefs take root in your mind by becoming automatic thoughts—those that arise without conscious effort. They are often self-reinforcing, meaning that the more you believe something, the more you unconsciously act in ways that confirm that belief.

This creates a cycle where limiting beliefs continue to shape your behavior and choices, leading to a restricted view of what you can achieve. The cumulative impact on your behavior, decision-making, and overall satisfaction with life can be profound, as these beliefs often prevent you from taking risks, pursuing opportunities, or even acknowledging your own strengths and successes.

Common Self-Defeating Thoughts

Self-defeating thoughts are a common manifestation of limiting beliefs, and they often reflect a negative view of yourself and your abilities. These thoughts can take many forms, but some of the most pervasive include beliefs like *"I'm not good enough," "I can't change my situation,"* and *"The world is against me."* Each of these thoughts fuels the victim mentality by reinforcing the idea that you are powerless to change your circumstances.

These thoughts perpetuate feelings of powerlessness and helplessness by focusing your attention on what you perceive as your weaknesses or limitations rather than your strengths and possibilities. For example, the belief that *"I'm not good enough"* can prevent you from even attempting new challenges, assuming you will fail even before you begin.

Similarly, thinking *"I can't change my situation"* can lead to inaction, as you believe any effort to improve your circumstances would be useless. Over time, these thoughts can become self-fulfilling prophecies, where your ingrained belief in your limitations leads you to act in ways that ensure you remain stuck in the same patterns, never realizing your full potential.

How to Identify Limiting Beliefs

To overcome limiting beliefs, you first need to identify them, which requires deep self-reflection. One effective method is to engage in guided exercises specifically designed to uncover these deeply rooted beliefs.

For example, you might start by asking yourself questions like, *"What do I believe about my abilities?"* or *"What fears hold me back from pursuing my goals?"* These questions can help bring unconscious beliefs to the surface, where they can be examined more critically.

Journaling is another powerful tool for identifying negative thought patterns. By writing down your thoughts and emotions regularly, you can start to notice recurring themes and beliefs that may be influencing your behavior. The mere process of putting thoughts into words can help clarify vague or subconscious beliefs, making them easier to challenge and change.

Mindfulness practices, such as meditation, can also play a crucial role in identifying limiting beliefs. By cultivating a state of non-judgmental awareness, you can observe your thoughts as they arise without immediately accepting them as truth. This allows you to see your thoughts more objectively and recognize when you are engaging in self-defeating patterns.

Once these beliefs are identified, it's important to question their origin and validity. Ask yourself whether these beliefs are based on solid facts or assumptions you have accepted without evidence.

Consider where these beliefs came from—were they imposed by others, or did they develop from a specific experience? By carefully scrutinizing these thoughts, you can begin to dismantle the limiting beliefs that have been holding you back.

Cultivating Self-Awareness

Self-awareness is a cornerstone of personal growth and a key factor in overcoming the victim mentality. By becoming more attuned to your thoughts, emotions, and behaviors, you can begin to identify the patterns that have been holding you back.

In this section, we will discuss the importance of self-awareness in recognizing automatic reactions, how mindfulness can enhance your understanding of these patterns, and the role of reflective practices in deepening your insight. Developing self-awareness empowers you to take control of your mindset and make intentional choices that lead to positive change.

The Role of Self-Awareness

Self-awareness is the ability to observe and understand your own thoughts, emotions, and behaviors with clarity. It plays a vital role in personal growth because it allows you to recognize the automatic reactions and thought patterns that often go unnoticed yet significantly impact your life.

When you develop self-awareness, you notice how specific thoughts trigger emotional responses, influencing your actions. For example, if you habitually think, *"I can't do this,"* every time you face a challenge, self-awareness allows you to catch that thought before it undermines your efforts. By becoming aware of these patterns, you gain the power to change them, breaking the cycle of negativity that sustains the victim mentality.

Furthermore, self-awareness is closely linked to emotional intelligence, which is the ability to understand and manage your emotions effectively. When you are self-aware, you can identify your emotions as they arise rather than being controlled by them. This awareness enables you to respond to situations more thoughtfully, rather than reacting impulsively based on ingrained habits.

For instance, instead of reacting with frustration when faced with a setback, self-awareness allows you to pause, recognize your feelings, and choose a better response. This ability to manage your emotions is crucial for personal growth, as it helps you navigate challenges with resilience and maintain a positive, proactive mindset.

Developing Mindfulness Practices

Mindfulness is a practice that enhances self-awareness by focusing your attention on the present moment. It involves observing your thoughts, emotions, and physical sensations without judgment, which helps you gain insight into your mental and emotional processes.

One of the most effective ways to develop mindfulness is through meditation, where you sit quietly and focus on your breath or a specific thought. This practice trains your mind to stay present and observe thoughts as they come and go, rather than becoming entangled in them.

Another powerful mindfulness technique is breathwork, which involves controlling your breathing to calm the mind and body. By focusing on your breath, you can anchor yourself in the present moment, reducing anxiety and creating space for clearer thinking. Body scans are also an effective mindfulness practice, where you systematically focus on different parts of your body, noticing any sensations without trying to change them. This practice helps you connect with your physical self and become more aware of how your emotions manifest in your body.

Mindfulness helps you observe your thoughts and emotions from a distance, which is essential for self-awareness. When you practice mindfulness regularly, you become more attuned to your internal processes and can recognize patterns that might otherwise go unnoticed. For instance, you might notice that you tend to think negatively about yourself whenever you make a mistake. With mindfulness, you can observe this thought without judgment and then decide how to respond to it, rather than automatically falling into a negative spiral.

Reflective Practices to Enhance Self-Awareness

Reflective practices are another powerful way to deepen self-awareness. Journaling, for instance, allows you to explore your thoughts, emotions, and experiences in writing, which can help you uncover patterns and beliefs that influence your behavior. By regularly documenting your thoughts, you can see connections between your emotions and actions, gaining deeper insights into your internal world. For example, you might notice that you feel anxious whenever you face a new challenge, leading you to avoid these situations. By reflecting on this pattern, you can start to question why you react this way and explore ways to change your response.

To enhance your journaling practice, consider using specific questions and prompts that encourage introspection. For example, ask yourself, *"What beliefs are driving my decisions today?"* or *"How did I react to challenges this week, and what can I learn from those reactions?"* These prompts can help you focus your reflection and dig deeper into the underlying causes of your thoughts and behaviors.

Setting aside regular time for self-reflection is essential for tracking your progress and growth. Whether through journaling, meditation, or quiet contemplation, consistent reflection allows you to monitor changes in your thoughts and behaviors over time. This ongoing practice helps you become more aware of how you are evolving, providing a clear picture of your personal development journey. By regularly assessing your progress, you can identify areas where you've made positive changes and where further work is needed, ensuring that you stay on track toward your goals.

The Power of Perspective

Perspective shapes how we experience and interpret the world around us. The way you choose to view your circumstances can either limit your potential or open up new possibilities for growth and empowerment. In this section, we'll explore the profound impact that perspective has on your mindset and how shifting your outlook can transform challenges into opportunities. By understanding and practicing techniques like cognitive reframing and adopting a growth-oriented mindset, you can learn to see your experiences in a new light, moving away from the constraints of a victim mentality and toward a more empowered and resilient approach to life.

Shifting Your Perspective to Empowerment

Perspective is the lens through which you view the world, and it plays a critical role in shaping your reality and experiences. How you interpret events and circumstances can limit your potential or empower you to overcome challenges.

When you adopt a negative or victim-oriented perspective, you are tempted to feel powerless, trapped by your circumstances, and unable to make meaningful changes in your life. This perspective keeps you focused on obstacles rather than possibilities, reinforcing the belief that you have little control over your destiny.

The concept of "reframing" involves changing the way you perceive a situation to see it in a more positive or constructive light. Reframing doesn't mean ignoring the difficulties or pretending that challenges don't exist; instead, it's about shifting your focus from what's wrong to what can be learned or gained from the experience.

> *"I never lose. I either win or learn."*
> — Nelson Mandela

For example, instead of viewing a failure as a sign of your inadequacy, you can reframe it as a valuable learning experience that provides insight into how to improve in the future. By actively choosing to see situations as opportunities for growth, you empower yourself to take control of your life and move beyond the limitations of a victim mentality.

Practical examples of reframing might include seeing a job loss not as a devastating end, but as a chance to explore new career paths that align more closely with your passions. Another example could be viewing criticism not as a personal attack, but as constructive feedback that can help you grow and develop your skills. These shifts in perspective can significantly change your emotional response to situations, turning what might initially seem like setbacks into stepping stones for personal and professional growth.

The Role of Cognitive Reframing

Cognitive reframing is a psychological technique that helps you alter your perception of situations, leading to more positive and empowering outcomes. This process involves three key steps: 1) identifying the negative or limiting thought; 2) challenging its accuracy and usefulness, and 3) replacing it with a more balanced and empowering belief.

To begin practicing cognitive reframing, first identify the specific thought that is contributing to your feelings of helplessness or negativity. For instance, you might notice a recurring thought like, *"I always fail at everything I try."* Once identified, the next step is to challenge this thought by questioning whether it's truly accurate. Consider the evidence—ask yourself: *"Are there instances where you have succeeded?"* *"Am I generalizing one failure to all aspects of my life?"* By critically examining the thought, you can begin to see its flaws and recognize that it may not be as valid as you initially believed.

The final step is to replace the limiting thought with a more empowering one. Instead of thinking, *"I always fail at everything,"* you might reframe it to, *"I've faced challenges before, but I've also had successes. I can learn from my mistakes and improve."* This new belief provides a more accurate reflection of reality and encourages a proactive approach to future challenges.

Consistency is essential for solidifying new perspectives. Just like any habit, the more you practice, the more natural it becomes to view situations from a positive and empowering angle. Over time, cognitive reframing can help you develop a mindset that is resilient, adaptive, and open to growth, allowing you to move beyond the constraints of a victim mentality.

Embracing a Growth-Oriented Perspective

The difference between a fixed mindset and a growth mindset is also fundamental to understanding how perspective influences your ability to overcome challenges. A fixed mindset is characterized by the belief that your abilities, intelligence, and talents are static and unchangeable. People with a fixed mindset tend to avoid challenges, give up easily when faced with obstacles, and view effort as fruitless. This mindset aligns closely with the victim mentality, as it fosters a sense of helplessness and resignation in the face of difficulties.

In contrast, a growth mindset is based on the belief that your abilities can be developed and improved through effort, learning, and perseverance. This perspective encourages you to see challenges as opportunities to grow rather than as threats to your self-worth. When you adopt a growth mindset, you are more likely to embrace new experiences, persist in the face of setbacks, and learn from your mistakes.

Adopting a growth mindset can be a powerful tool in overcoming the victim mentality. By focusing on learning, growth, and resilience, you shift your perspective from one of limitation to one of possibility. This shift empowers you to take control of your development and helps you build the mental and emotional resilience needed to navigate life's challenges effectively.

Encouraging a growth-oriented perspective involves consciously focusing on progress rather than perfection, valuing effort over innate ability, and embracing the idea that failure is a natural part of the learning process. By cultivating this mindset, you equip yourself with the tools to move beyond a victim mentality and toward a life of empowerment, achievement, and continuous personal growth.

In the next chapter, we'll continue our discussion by focusing on the critical aspects of taking ownership of your life by embracing personal responsibility, setting boundaries, and cultivating resilience and adaptability. These components are essential to breaking free from the victim mentality and building a life rooted in courage, authenticity, and self-ownership.

Chapter 5

Taking Ownership of Your Life

"Faith is taking the first step even when you don't see the whole staircase."
— Martin Luther King, Jr.

T RUE EMPOWERMENT BEGINS WITH taking full responsibility for your actions, decisions, and the direction of your life. This chapter examines what it means to take ownership of your life, and how embracing personal responsibility leads to greater freedom and control. By setting healthy boundaries, asserting yourself confidently, and cultivating resilience, you will start to break free from the limitations of the victim mentality and create a life that reflects your true potential.

Embracing Personal Responsibility

Embracing personal responsibility is the foundation of true empowerment. It means acknowledging that you can influence your life's outcomes through your choices and actions. This shift in mindset moves you away from blaming external factors for your current situation and toward taking control of your own fate.

This section will discuss the importance of accepting responsibility for your life, the obstacles that often prevent people from doing so, and the transformation this approach can have on your personal growth and overall well-being. By learning to set clear boundaries, assert your needs, and hold yourself accountable, you can start to unlock your true potential and create a life more aligned with your values and goals.

Understanding Personal Responsibility

Personal responsibility is the recognition and acceptance that you are solely accountable for your actions, decisions, and the outcomes of your life. It means acknowledging that, while you may not control every external circumstance, you do have control over how you respond to those circumstances. This involves taking ownership of your choices, behaviors, and mindset, rather than attributing them solely to external factors.

Personal responsibility is not about blaming yourself for everything that happens; instead, it's about understanding the power you have to influence your life through your decisions and actions. By embracing personal responsibility, you shift from a passive stance—where life happens to you—to an active role, where you shape your own destiny.

Overcoming Blame and Excuses

Blame and excuses are common defense mechanisms that people use to avoid taking responsibility for their actions. When things go wrong, it's often easier to point fingers at others rather than face the discomfort of acknowledging our own role in the situation.

This pattern of blame and excuse-making is a hallmark of the victim mentality, as it allows you to avoid accountability and maintain the belief that you are powerless to change your circumstances. However, this mindset ultimately keeps you stuck, as it prevents you from learning from your experiences and making the necessary changes to improve your life.

The psychological reasons behind blame-shifting are often rooted in fear—fear of failure, fear of rejection, or fear of not being good enough. By blaming others or making excuses, you protect yourself from these fears, but at the cost of your growth and empowerment.

To overcome this tendency, it's important to interrupt the blame cycle and redirect your focus toward finding solutions. This might involve asking yourself questions like, *"What could I have done differently?"* or *"What can I learn from this experience?"* By shifting your focus from blame to constructive problem-solving, you take the first step toward embracing personal responsibility.

The Power of Self-Accountability

Self-accountability is another powerful tool for personal growth and empowerment. When you hold yourself accountable for your actions and decisions, you reinforce the belief that you are in control of your life. Accountability cultivates a sense of ownership and responsibility, which is paramount for breaking free from the victim mentality. Self-accountability involves regularly evaluating your progress, acknowledging your mistakes, and making adjustments as needed to stay focused on reaching your goals.

In addition to self-accountability, getting help from external accountability partners—such as mentors, coaches, or trusted friends—can provide needed support and encouragement. They can help you stay committed to your goals, offer constructive feedback, and challenge you to push beyond your comfort zone. By involving others in your journey, you increase your chances of success and build a network of support that reinforces your commitment to personal growth.

To build responsibility and self-ownership, it's also important to set clear, achievable goals and monitor your progress regularly. This might involve breaking larger goals into smaller, manageable steps, setting deadlines, and reviewing your progress on a weekly or monthly basis. By setting and achieving goals, you strengthen your sense of accountability and reinforce the belief that you are capable of making positive changes in your life.

Setting Healthy Boundaries and Asserting Yourself

Setting and maintaining healthy boundaries is essential for protecting your well-being and ensuring your needs are respected in all areas of life. Without clear boundaries, you'll more than likely feel overwhelmed, taken advantage of, or unable to say no, which can reinforce a sense of powerlessness.

In this section, we'll talk about why establishing healthy boundaries is so important, how to identify areas where they are needed, and the techniques for asserting yourself confidently. By learning to set and enforce boundaries, you reclaim your personal power and build relationships based on mutual respect and understanding.

The Importance of Healthy Boundaries

Boundaries are the limits you set to protect your personal space, values, and well-being in both personal and professional relationships. They define what you are willing to accept from others and how you expect to be treated. Healthy boundaries are essential for maintaining your sense of self-respect and ensuring that your needs are met.

When boundaries are weak (i.e., vague, not enforced, or even non-existent), you may find yourself agreeing to things that make you uncomfortable, overextending yourself, or allowing others to take advantage of you. This lack of boundaries can contribute to the victim mentality, as it perpetuates feelings of powerlessness and resentment.

Establishing and maintaining clear, healthy boundaries helps you to take control of your interactions and relationships. Boundaries clearly communicate your needs and limits, which helps prevent misunderstandings and conflicts. Setting healthy boundaries also protects your mental and emotional well-being by ensuring that you are not overburdened or disrespected by others. When you consistently enforce your boundaries, you build a foundation of self-respect and create relationships that are mutually beneficial.

Finding Areas Where Boundaries Are Needed

Identifying areas in your life where boundaries are lacking is the first step toward establishing them. To do this, start by reflecting on situations where you feel uncomfortable, stressed, or resentful. These feelings often indicate that your boundaries are being violated or that you must set clearer limits. Activities like journaling about recent interactions that left you feeling drained or frustrated can help you pinpoint specific areas where boundaries are needed.

Common situations where boundaries are necessary include the workplace, family dynamics, friendships, and romantic relationships. In the workplace, you might need to set boundaries around your time, such as not answering work phone calls or emails after hours.

In family or friendships, boundaries might involve limiting discussions on topics that are known to cause conflict or saying no to requests that overextend you. Recognizing the signs that your boundaries are being violated—such as feeling guilty for saying no, feeling overwhelmed, or being taken for granted—can help you identify where changes are needed.

Techniques for Asserting Yourself

Once you've identified where boundaries are needed, the next step is to assert yourself by communicating those boundaries clearly and confidently. Assertiveness involves expressing your needs and limits in a way that is firm but respectful. It's important to strike a balance between aggression and passivity—being too aggressive can lead to conflict, while being too passive can result in your boundaries being ignored.

Practical strategies for assertive communication include using "I" statements to express how you feel and what you need, such as *"I need some time to myself after work, so I won't be available for calls in the evening."* Another technique is to be direct and specific about your boundaries, avoiding vague language that could lead to misunderstandings. For example, instead of saying, *"I'm too busy,"* you might say, *"I'm not available to take on additional tasks this week."*

Assertiveness is vital for reclaiming power and self-respect. By standing up for your needs and enforcing your boundaries, you reinforce the message that your time, energy, and well-being are valuable. However, it's also important to be prepared for pushback from others who may be accustomed to overstepping your boundaries.

Handling this resistance requires staying firm in your decisions, reiterating your boundaries as needed, and not giving in to guilt or pressure. With practice, asserting yourself becomes easier, and you'll find that maintaining healthy boundaries leads to more balanced and fulfilling relationships.

Cultivate Resilience and Adaptability

Resilience and adaptability are essential qualities that help you to navigate life's challenges with strength and flexibility. While setbacks and difficulties are inevitable, your ability to recover, learn, and adjust determines how successfully you move forward.

In this section, we will explore the importance of building resilience to overcome obstacles, and how adaptability allows you to thrive in changing circumstances. By cultivating these qualities, you can maintain a sense of control and optimism, even in the face of adversity, and continue to grow and succeed in your journey toward personal empowerment.

Understanding Resilience

Resilience is the ability to bounce back from setbacks, adapt to change, and keep going in the face of adversity. It is a crucial trait for overcoming challenges and maintaining a positive outlook, even when life gets tough. Resilience is closely linked to a growth mindset, where you see challenges as opportunities to learn and grow rather than as insurmountable obstacles. The more resilient you are, the better equipped you are to handle difficulties without being overwhelmed. Resilience is not something you either have or don't have—it's a quality that can be developed and strengthened over time through intentional practices and mindset shifts.

Building Mental and Emotional Strength

Building mental and emotional strength is crucial for resilience and adaptability. This process involves developing the inner resources that enable you to face challenges, manage stress, and maintain a positive outlook even in difficult circumstances. Here are some ways to develop both mental toughness and emotional intelligence:

Mental Toughness: Developing a Strong Mindset

1. Positive Self-Talk

What is Positive Self-Talk? Positive self-talk is the practice of consciously replacing negative, self-defeating thoughts with affirming and empowering ones. The way you talk to yourself directly impacts your mental strength. Negative self-talk can erode your confidence and resilience, while positive self-talk can bolster your mental toughness and help you face challenges with a constructive attitude.

Practicing Positive Self-Talk: Start by becoming aware of your inner dialogue. When you catch yourself thinking negatively, pause and reframe those thoughts. For instance, if you find yourself thinking, *"I can't handle this,"* reframe it to, *"This is difficult, but I can find a way through it."* Over time, this practice can help shift your mindset from one of doubt and defeat to one of confidence and capability.

2. Visualization Techniques

The Power of Visualization: Visualization involves mentally rehearsing or imagining a successful outcome to a situation before it happens. This technique is widely used by athletes, performers, and high achievers to build confidence and prepare mentally for challenges. By visualizing a successful outcome, you strengthen your belief in your ability to achieve your goals and navigate obstacles.

How to Practice Visualization: Find a quiet space, close your eyes, and vividly imagine yourself successfully overcoming a challenge or achieving a goal. Engage all your senses in the process—see, hear, and feel what it means to succeed. Regularly practicing visualization helps condition your mind to expect and strive for positive outcomes, enhancing mental resilience.

3. Stress Management Strategies

Importance of Managing Stress: Chronic stress can deplete your mental resources, making it harder to stay resilient in the face of adversity. Learning to manage stress effectively is crucial for mental toughness. When you are able to keep stress under control, you can think more clearly, make better decisions, and maintain your focus even under pressure.

Techniques for Managing Stress:

- *Deep Breathing Exercises:* Practice deep breathing techniques, such as diaphragmatic breathing, where you breathe deeply into your abdomen rather than shallowly into your chest. This activates the body's relaxation response, helping to reduce stress and calm your mind.

- *Mindfulness Meditation:* Engage in mindfulness meditation to increase your awareness of the present moment and reduce stress. By focusing on your breath or a specific sensation, you can calm your mind and prevent it from being overwhelmed by stressors.

- *Physical Activity:* Regular physical activity is one of the most effective ways to manage stress. Exercise releases endorphins, which are natural mood enhancers, and helps reduce the effects of stress on your body and mind.

Emotional Intelligence: Strengthening Emotional Resilience

1. Understanding and Managing Emotions

The Role of Emotional Intelligence: Emotional intelligence (EI) is the ability to recognize, understand, and manage your own emotions, as well as to recognize and influence the emotions of others. High EI is a key component of emotional resilience, enabling you to handle emotional challenges with greater ease and effectiveness.

Developing Emotional Awareness: Start by regularly checking in with yourself to identify what emotions you are feeling. Labeling your emotions accurately (e.g., *"I'm feeling anxious"* rather than *"I'm not feeling well"*) can help you gain a clearer understanding of your emotional state. This awareness is the first step in managing your emotions effectively.

Managing Emotional Responses: Once you've identified your emotions, practice strategies to manage them constructively. For example, if you're feeling overwhelmed, you might practice deep breathing to calm yourself, or if you're angry, you might take a moment to step back and cool down before responding. Over time, these practices can help you maintain emotional balance in challenging situations.

2. Cultivating Emotional Balance

Building Emotional Resilience: Emotional balance involves maintaining a stable and grounded emotional state, even when faced with stress or adversity. It's about being able to experience emotions fully without being controlled by them. By cultivating emotional balance, you enhance your ability to respond to challenges in a calm and composed manner.

Techniques for Emotional Balance:

- *Mindfulness Practices:* Regular mindfulness practices like meditation or yoga can help you stay centered and balanced. These practices encourage you to observe your emotions without judgment, reducing the likelihood that strong feelings will dominate your thinking.

- *Journaling:* Writing about your emotions in a journal can help you process and release them. It provides a safe space to explore your feelings and gain insights into emotional patterns that may be affecting your resilience.

- *Seeking Social Support:* Building and maintaining strong relationships with friends, family, or support groups can provide emotional support during tough times. Sharing your experiences with others who understand can help you manage your emotions more effectively.

3. Building Resilience Through Emotional Intelligence

Connecting Emotional Intelligence to Resilience: Emotional intelligence contributes to resilience by enabling you to manage your emotional responses, empathize with others, and navigate social complexities. When you have strong EI, you are better equipped to handle stress, resolve conflicts, and maintain positive relationships, all of which are essential for resilience.

Practicing Empathy: Empathy, the ability to understand and share the feelings of others, is a crucial aspect of emotional intelligence. Practicing empathy can improve your relationships and give you a broader perspective on challenges, helping you build resilience. For example, when facing a conflict, try to see the situation from the other person's point of view. This can help you manage your own emotions and respond more constructively.

By focusing on building both mental toughness and emotional intelligence, you can greatly enhance your resilience. These skills will empower you to face life's challenges with greater confidence, adaptability, and strength, ensuring that you can navigate difficult situations while maintaining a positive and proactive mindset.

Developing Adaptability

Adaptability is the ability to adjust your thinking and behavior in response to changing circumstances. In a constantly-evolving world, adaptability is essential for navigating life's uncertainties while maintaining a sense of control. Being adaptable means being open to new ideas, willing to change course when necessary, and able to approach problems from different angles.

To improve your adaptability, embrace change rather than resist it. This might require seeing change as an opportunity for growth rather than a threat to stability. Problem-solving skills are also key to adaptability; when faced with a challenge, try to view it as a puzzle to be solved rather than a roadblock to be avoided. Creative thinking exercises, such as brainstorming multiple solutions to a problem or approaching a situation from a different perspective, can also help you become more flexible in your thinking.

Practical ways to develop adaptability may include putting yourself in new situations that challenge your usual way of thinking, practicing flexibility in your daily routines, and regularly reflecting on how you handle change. By building adaptability, you increase your ability to thrive in a variety of circumstances, making you more resilient and empowered to handle whatever life throws your way.

In the next chapter, we'll discuss cultivating empowerment by developing a growth mindset, practicing self-compassion and forgiveness, and building a sense of agency and control. These skills are crucial for transitioning from a victim mentality to a mindset of empowerment and self-ownership.

Chapter 6
The Journey to Empowerment

"The first step in empowerment is taking control of your health, respecting yourself and understanding and celebrating the value you bring to your family and society."

— Milind Soman

E MPOWERMENT IS THE PROCESS of taking control of your life, recognizing your worth, and making decisions that align with your values and goals. It's about moving beyond limitations, embracing your strengths, and shaping the life you want to live. In this chapter, you'll learn how to develop a growth mindset, practice self-compassion and forgiveness, and build a sense of agency and control. By cultivating empowerment, you can transform your mindset and take meaningful steps toward achieving your full potential.

Developing a Growth Mindset

A growth mindset is the belief that your abilities and intelligence can be developed through effort, learning, and perseverance.

This mindset contrasts with a fixed mindset, where individuals believe their talents and abilities are static and unchangeable.

In this section, we will explore the transformative power of adopting a growth mindset and how it can help you overcome obstacles, embrace challenges, and continuously improve. By developing a growth mindset, you'll open yourself up to new possibilities and take steps toward achieving your goals.

Understanding the Growth Mindset

A growth mindset is the belief that your abilities, intelligence, and talents are not fixed traits but can be developed over time. This is a stark contrast to a fixed mindset, where individuals believe that their qualities are innate and unchangeable. People with a fixed mindset often avoid challenges, give up easily, and view effort as fruitless. They may also feel threatened by the success of others, believing that it diminishes their own worth.

On the other hand, a growth mindset encourages continuous learning, resilience, and a positive attitude toward effort. People with a growth mindset see challenges as opportunities to grow, embrace failures as part of the learning process, and are inspired by the success of others because it shows them what is possible. They understand that abilities can be cultivated and that intelligence is not a static trait but something that can be enhanced through dedication and hard work.

Let's get here!

GROWTH MINDSET
"Failure is an opportunity to grow"
"I can learn to do anything I want"
"Challenges help me to grow"
"My effort and attitude determine my abilities"
"Feedback is constructive"
"I am inspired by the success of others"
"I like to try new things"

FIXED MINDSET
"Failure is the limit of my abilities"
"I'm either good at it or I'm not"
"My abilities are unchanging"
"I don't like to be challenged"
"I can either do it, or I can't"
"My potential is predetermined"
"When I'm frustrated, I give up"
"Feedback and criticism are personal"
"I stick to what I know"

The connection between a growth mindset and overcoming the victim mentality is profound. When you believe that your circumstances can improve and that you have the power to change your life through your actions, you are far less likely to feel like a victim of circumstances. Instead of feeling trapped by limitations, you begin to see possibilities for growth and change, even in difficult situations. This shift in perspective is crucial for breaking free from the constraints of a victim mentality and moving toward a life of empowerment and personal agency.

Shifting from a Fixed to a Growth Mindset

Transitioning from a fixed mindset to a growth mindset is a process that requires self-awareness, deliberate effort, and ongoing practice. The first step is to identify the fixed mindset beliefs that may be holding you back. These beliefs often manifest as self-defeating thoughts like, *"I'm just not good at this," "I'll never be able to change,"* or *"There's no point in trying because I'll fail anyway."* Such thoughts limit your potential by discouraging effort and making you feel as though your abilities are set in stone.

Once you've identified these limiting beliefs, the next step is to challenge them. Ask yourself, *"Is this belief really true?"* or *"What evidence do I have that contradicts this belief?"* For example, if you believe that you're *"not good at math,"* consider the times when you've successfully solved a math problem or learned a new concept. Recognizing that your abilities have improved in the past can help you see that they can continue to improve with practice and effort.

Reframing fixed mindset thoughts is an essential part of this process. Instead of thinking, *"I'm not good at this,"* reframe it to, *"I'm still learning, and I can get better with practice."* Instead of saying, *"I'll never be able to change,"* try, *"Change takes time and effort, but I can make progress."* This shift in language is powerful because it opens up possibilities for growth and encourages you to take action rather than resigning yourself to limitations.

To foster a growth mindset, it's also important to actively seek out and embrace challenges. Rather than avoiding tasks that seem difficult, view them as opportunities to stretch your abilities and learn something new. When you encounter obstacles, remember that struggle is a natural part of the learning process and that persistence is key to overcoming difficulties. Celebrate your efforts, regardless of the outcome, because effort is the foundation of growth.

Learning from criticism is another crucial aspect of developing a growth mindset. Instead of viewing criticism as a personal attack, see it as a valuable feedback mechanism to help you improve. Ask for feedback from others, and use it as a tool to refine your skills and strategies. This approach helps you grow and promotes resilience as you become less afraid of making mistakes or facing setbacks.

TIP: When facing challenges and setbacks, remember that struggle is a natural part of the learning process and that persistence is key to overcoming difficulties.

Finally, recognize and celebrate effort and progress, not just results. When you focus solely on outcomes, you may miss the value of the learning process. Acknowledge the hard work you've put in, even if the results aren't perfect. This reinforces the idea that growth is a journey, and every step forward is an achievement.

Applying the Growth Mindset Daily

Integrating a growth mindset into your daily life requires consistent practice and a commitment to viewing challenges as opportunities. One way is to set small, achievable goals that encourage progress rather than perfection. For example, if you're learning a new skill, break it down into manageable steps and celebrate each milestone along the way. This approach keeps you motivated and helps you see how your efforts are leading to improvement over time.

When you encounter setbacks, practice viewing them as learning opportunities. Instead of seeing a mistake as a failure, ask yourself, *"What can I learn from this experience?"* and *"How can I apply this lesson in the future?"* This mindset shift helps you bounce back from setbacks more quickly and with a greater sense of purpose.

Incorporating positive self-talk into your daily routine is another powerful way to reinforce a growth mindset. Replace negative, limiting thoughts with affirmations that encourage growth and resilience. For instance, if you find yourself thinking, *"I'm not good enough,"* counter it with, *"I'm improving every day, and I'm proud of my progress."* This practice helps build confidence and reinforces the belief that you can develop your abilities over time.

Another practical application of the growth mindset is to actively seek out opportunities for learning and development.

This might involve taking on new challenges at work, pursuing further education, or engaging in activities that push you out of your comfort zone. By regularly exposing yourself to new experiences, you not only build your skills but also strengthen your belief in your ability to grow and adapt.

Strive for progress rather than perfection in all areas of life. Whether working on a personal project, developing a new habit, or striving toward a long-term goal, remember that growth is a gradual process. Celebrate the small wins and recognize that each step forward brings you closer to your ultimate goals.

Finally, understand that a growth mindset is not just about personal development—it can transform your relationships, career, and overall outlook on life. When you apply a growth mindset to your interactions with others, you become more open to collaboration, more willing to share knowledge, and more empathetic to others' struggles. In your career, a growth mindset can drive innovation, creativity, and a willingness to take risks, all of which are essential for success. In life, this mindset helps you maintain a positive, proactive approach to challenges, allowing you to navigate difficulties with confidence and resilience.

By consistently applying the principles of a growth mindset daily, you create a foundation for continuous improvement and long-term success. This mindset not only helps you overcome the limitations of a victim mentality but also keeps you focused on achieving your full potential.

In the next chapter, we'll examine how to overcome obstacles by dealing with setbacks and failures, managing fear and self-doubt, and seeking support to build resilience.

Chapter 7

Overcoming Challenges, Setbacks and Failures

"You should never view your challenges as a disadvantage. Instead, it's important for you to understand that your experience facing and overcoming adversity is actually one of your biggest advantages."
— Michelle Obama

LIFE WILL ALWAYS BE filled with challenges and setbacks, but how you approach these obstacles can make all the difference in your journey toward empowerment. In this chapter, we will explore strategies for overcoming the hurdles that can stand in your way, whether they are external barriers or internal struggles.

Dealing with Setbacks and Failures

Setbacks and failures are an inevitable part of life, but they don't have to define your journey or limit your potential. How you respond to these challenges can either hold you back or propel you forward. In this section, we will see the importance of viewing setbacks as opportunities for learning and growth rather than as insurmountable obstacles. By adopting a resilient mindset, embracing the lessons that failures offer, and staying committed to your goals, you can turn even the most difficult experiences into stepping stones toward success.

The Role of Setbacks and Failures

Setbacks and failures are an inevitable part of any personal or professional journey. No matter how meticulously you plan or how much effort you invest, there will be times when things just don't go as anticipated. Accepting this reality is the first step in developing a resilient mindset. It's important to recognize that setbacks and failures are not reflections of your overall worth or potential; rather, they are natural occurrences that everyone experiences.

Failures and setbacks serve as valuable feedback mechanisms. They provide you with critical insights that you might not have gained otherwise. These experiences can be seen as opportunities to learn and grow rather than as reasons to give up. By viewing setbacks as temporary hurdles instead of permanent roadblocks, you can begin to approach them with a mindset focused on growth and improvement.

Moreover, differentiating between temporary setbacks and what might seem like permanent failures is crucial. Often, what feels like a failure is merely a setback that requires a different approach or more time. Reframing your perspective to see failures as part of the learning process allows you to continue pursuing your goals with renewed determination and insight.

> **TIP:** Remember that setbacks and failures do not reflect your overall worth or potential; rather, they are natural occurrences that everyone experiences.

Shifting Perspective on Setbacks

Your perspective on setbacks plays a significant role in how you respond to them. If you view setbacks as insurmountable obstacles, they can easily overwhelm you, leading to discouragement and a loss of motivation. However, by reframing setbacks as challenges to be overcome, you can change how you interact with these difficulties. This powerful mindset shift turns setbacks from sources of frustration into opportunities to develop resilience, creativity, and problem-solving skills.

Resilience is the ability to bounce back from adversity, and it's a trait that can be developed through intentional practice. When faced with a setback, rather than focusing on the disappointment or frustration, ask yourself what you can learn from the experience.

Consider how the setback might be an opportunity to refine your approach or develop new skills. For example, if a business venture fails, it might be a chance to reassess your market strategy, improve your product, or learn more about your target audience. By focusing on what you can gain from the experience, you shift your energy from dwelling on the negative to actively finding ways to grow and improve.

"No problem can be solved from the same level of consciousness that created it"
— Albert Einstein

Resilience is not just about bouncing back; it's also about learning to manage challenges with grace and adaptability. When you encounter setbacks, it's natural to feel disappointed or frustrated. However, by practicing mindfulness and staying present, you can process these emotions more constructively, preventing them from derailing your progress. Instead of allowing a setback to define you, use it as a stepping stone to build greater emotional strength and adaptability.

Strategies for Managing Setbacks

Managing setbacks requires a proactive and structured approach. The first step is to pause and evaluate the situation objectively. It's easy to get caught up in emotions when things go wrong, but taking a step back to assess the situation can provide clarity. Ask yourself questions like: *"What specifically went wrong?" "Why did it happen?" "Were there external factors beyond my control, or were there internal factors I could have addressed?"* This focused analysis helps you understand the root causes of the setback and provides valuable insights for future actions.

Once you have a clear understanding of what went wrong, it's time to develop a plan to address the problem. This plan should include setting new, realistic goals that are aligned with your current situation. For instance, if you've encountered a setback in your career, such as not getting a promotion, your new goals might involve acquiring additional skills, seeking feedback, or exploring other opportunities that align with your long-term career objectives. Adjusting your strategies to reflect the lessons learned from the setback is key to moving forward. This might involve changing your approach, seeking out new resources, or taking a different path altogether.

Another critical component of managing setbacks is building a support system. No one succeeds entirely on their own, and having a network of supportive individuals can make a significant difference in how you navigate challenges. Your support system might include friends, family, mentors, colleagues, or even professional advisors who can offer encouragement, advice, and a different perspective.

When setbacks occur, reaching out to your support network can provide emotional support and practical solutions. These individuals can help you see the situation from a different angle, suggest strategies you might not have considered, and remind you of your strengths and past successes.

Finally, it's important to remember that setbacks are not the end of the road but rather part of the journey. Every successful person has faced multiple failures and setbacks; what sets them apart is their ability to learn from these experiences and keep moving forward.

By maintaining a resilient mindset, focusing on growth, and leveraging your support system, you can turn setbacks into powerful opportunities for personal and professional development. This approach not only helps you overcome challenges but also strengthens your confidence and resolve, empowering you to achieve your goals despite the obstacles you encounter.

Managing Fear and Self-Doubt

Fear and self-doubt are powerful emotions that can hold you back from reaching your full potential. Whether it's the fear of failure, fear of judgment, or doubts about your abilities, these feelings can create significant obstacles on your path to success. However, it's important to recognize that fear and self-doubt are not insurmountable barriers—they are challenges that can be managed and overcome.

In this section, we'll examine sources of fear and self-doubt, understand their impact on decision-making and actions, and provide strategies for confronting these emotions head-on. By learning to manage fear and self-doubt rather than avoid them, you can build the confidence and resilience needed to pursue your goals with determination and clarity.

Identifying Sources of Fear and Self-Doubt

Fear and self-doubt are emotions that can significantly hinder your progress and keep you from reaching your full potential. These feelings often stem from various sources, such as the fear of failure, rejection, or the unknown. Understanding where these fears originate and how they impact your behavior is the first step in managing them effectively.

One of the most common fears contributing to a victim mentality is the fear of failure. This fear often arises from the belief that making mistakes is a reflection of your worth or capabilities. Consequently, you may avoid taking risks or pursuing opportunities because the possibility of failure feels too daunting. Similarly, the fear of rejection can prevent you from asserting yourself or taking chances in personal and professional relationships, rooted in concerns about how others perceive you and the potential pain of being judged or excluded.

Self-doubt, closely linked to these fears, undermines your confidence and decision-making abilities. When you doubt your capabilities, you're more likely to second-guess your choices, hesitate when opportunities arise, and ultimately miss out on experiences that could lead to greater growth. This doubt can create a cycle where your lack of confidence leads to inaction, which then reinforces your feelings of inadequacy.

The sources of fear and self-doubt often lie in past experiences and deeply ingrained limiting beliefs. If you've encountered failure or harsh criticism in the past, these experiences can shape how you view yourself and your abilities moving forward. For example, if you've been told repeatedly that you're not good at something, you may internalize this belief and carry it with you, allowing it to dictate your actions and decisions.

Techniques for Overcoming Fear

Once you've identified the sources of your fear and self-doubt, the next step is to actively confront and manage these emotions. Confronting fear involves directly addressing the things that hold you back. One effective technique is gradual exposure to the things you fear.

For example, if public speaking terrifies you, start by speaking in front of a small group of trusted friends. Over time, as you become more comfortable, you can gradually increase the size of your audience. This process, known as exposure therapy, helps to desensitize you to your fears and reduce their power over you.

Visualization is another powerful tool for managing fear. By mentally rehearsing a situation where you successfully confront a fear, you can build the confidence needed to face it in reality. Imagine yourself overcoming the challenge, feeling calm and confident, and achieving the outcome you desire. This practice can help shift your mindset from fear to empowerment.

Positive affirmations and constructive self-talk are crucial in reducing fear and boosting confidence. Replacing negative thoughts like *"I can't do this"* with affirmations such as *"I am capable and prepared to handle this challenge"* can rewire your thinking and strengthen your resolve. This shift in self-talk helps you approach challenges with a more positive and determined attitude.

Taking small, manageable steps is key to overcoming fear. You don't have to tackle your biggest fears all at once. Instead, take one at a time over a given timeframe. Remember, each small victory builds your confidence and reduces the grip that fear has over you. For instance, if you're afraid of failure in a particular area, start with tasks that carry low risk but still contribute to your growth. As you achieve success in these smaller areas, your confidence will grow, enabling you to take on larger challenges with greater confidence.

Building Confidence and Self-Efficacy

Confidence and self-efficacy are also essential for overcoming fear and self-doubt, as they empower you to take control of your life and pursue your goals.

Confidence, the belief in your ability to succeed, is critical in overcoming a victim mentality. When you believe in yourself, you're more likely to take risks, pursue opportunities, and persist in the face of challenges. Confidence empowers you to act rather than remain passive, which is crucial for breaking free from limiting beliefs.

Building confidence starts with setting small, realistic goals that you can achieve. Each accomplishment reinforces your belief in your abilities and provides a foundation for tackling more significant challenges. Celebrating your successes, no matter how small, is important because it reinforces positive behavior and builds momentum. Learning from your mistakes rather than fearing them also allows you to grow and improve, further boosting your confidence levels.

Self-efficacy, the belief in your ability to influence outcomes and make positive changes, is closely related to confidence but focuses more on your perceived ability to execute actions that lead to desired results. Building self-efficacy involves recognizing your past successes and using them as evidence of your capabilities. For example, if you've successfully completed a challenging project in the past, remind yourself of this achievement when facing a new challenge. This helps reinforce your belief that you can overcome obstacles and achieve your goals.

You can manage your emotions more effectively by addressing the sources of fear and self-doubt and actively working to build confidence and self-efficacy. This allows you to move beyond the boundaries of a victim mentality and embrace a mindset of empowerment and growth.

Seeking Support and Building Resilience

Resilience is the ability to recover from setbacks, adapt to change, and keep moving forward despite challenges. While resilience is a crucial trait for overcoming obstacles, it's not something you have to develop on your own.

Getting help from others can significantly enhance your resilience, providing you with the encouragement, perspective, and resources needed to navigate difficult times. Let's explore the importance of building a solid support network and see how it contributes to your ability to bounce back from adversity. Additionally, we'll discuss practical ways to strengthen your resilience, enabling you to face challenges with greater confidence and perseverance.

The Importance of Seeking Support

One key element in building resilience is recognizing when and why it's important to seek support from others. Life's challenges can be overwhelming when faced alone, and there is immense value in sharing your struggles with trusted friends, colleagues, or professionals who can offer guidance, perspective, and encouragement. Seeking support allows you to tap into a broader range of experiences and knowledge, helping you overcome obstacles more effectively.

It's important to overcome the stigma often associated with asking for help. Many people feel that seeking support is a sign of weakness or inadequacy, but in reality, it's a sign of strength. Acknowledging when you need help and being willing to reach out demonstrates self-awareness and a commitment to personal growth. Whether you turn to friends, family, mentors, or professional counselors, seeking support is an essential step in building resilience and moving forward with confidence.

Building a Resilient Support System

Developing a resilient support system is crucial for sustaining your ability to cope with challenges and setbacks. Start by identifying individuals in your life who offer positive, constructive support. These might include mentors, coaches, peers, or friends who understand your goals and are willing to provide encouragement and advice. Cultivating these relationships requires honesty and transparency about your struggles and being willing to reciprocate support when others need it.

Mentors, coaches, and therapists are particularly important in fostering resilience. They can offer valuable insights based on their knowledge and clinical insights, helping you navigate challenging situations more efficiently. Peer groups, whether in professional settings or personal circles, also provide a sense of community and shared understanding, which can be incredibly supportive. These groups create an environment where you can exchange ideas, learn from others, and gain the strength to persevere through challenges.

> **TIP:** Remember that acknowledging when you need help and being willing to reach out demonstrates self-awareness and a commitment to personal growth.

Maintaining strong, supportive connections requires effort and intentionality. Regular communication, mutual respect, and a willingness to invest time in these relationships are key. By nurturing these connections, you create a support network that not only helps you overcome immediate challenges but also contributes to your long-term growth and empowerment.

Cultivating Personal Resilience

While external support is invaluable, cultivating personal resilience is equally important. Resilience is the mental and emotional strength that allows you to recover from setbacks and adapt to changing circumstances. Developing this resilience involves a combination of mindfulness, stress management, and adaptability.

Mindfulness practices, such as meditation or deep breathing, help you stay present and grounded, reducing the impact of stress and anxiety. By managing stress effectively, you can approach challenges with a clearer mind and a more focused attitude. Adaptability, or the ability to adjust to new situations and challenges, is another key component of resilience. Embracing change rather than resisting it enables you to navigate uncertainties with greater ease and confidence.

Maintaining resilience, especially in the face of ongoing challenges, requires a proactive approach. This involves anticipating potential difficulties, preparing mentally and emotionally, and staying focused on your long-term goals. By regularly assessing your resilience levels and taking steps to strengthen them, you ensure that you are better equipped to handle whatever life throws your way.

In essence, the key to resilience is not just enduring tough times but thriving despite them. By seeking support, cultivating a strong support system, and developing personal resilience, you empower yourself to face challenges head-on and continue moving forward on your journey of growth and success.

In the next chapter, we'll talk about welcoming change and growth by stepping out of comfort zones, embracing uncertainty, and setting and pursuing meaningful goals. These skills are essential for breaking free from the victim mentality and building a mindset of continuous growth, resilience, and empowerment.

Chapter 8
Embracing Change and Growth

"Life begins at the end of your comfort zone."
— Neale Donald Walsch

C HANGE IS AN INEVITABLE part of life, and how you respond to it will be a determining factor in your personal and professional development. While change often brings uncertainty, it also presents opportunities for growth, learning, and personal transformation.

In this chapter, we will discuss the importance of embracing change with an open mind and a proactive attitude. By stepping out of your comfort zone and viewing change as a catalyst for growth, you can unlock new possibilities and move closer to achieving your full potential.

Stepping Out of Comfort Zones

Growth begins at the edge of your comfort zone. While it's natural to seek safety and familiarity, staying within the confines of what you know can limit your potential and hinder your progress. Stepping out of your comfort zone is essential for personal and professional development. In these moments of uncertainty and challenge, you discover new strengths, develop resilience, and gain the experiences necessary for growth.

This section will discuss the importance of pushing beyond your comfort zone, the benefits of embracing discomfort, and practical strategies for taking those first courageous steps into the unknown. By learning to navigate and thrive outside of your comfort zones, you can unlock new opportunities and continue evolving in ways you never thought possible.

Understanding the Comfort Zone

The concept of the *"comfort zone"* refers to a psychological state where you feel safe, secure, and at ease because you are sur-rounded by familiar environments, routines, and behaviors. In this state, you experience minimal stress and anxiety because you are not exposing yourself to new challenges or risks. While this might seem appealing, staying within your comfort zone can significantly affect your personal and professional development.

Staying within the comfort zone often reinforces the victim mentality, as it discourages you from taking the necessary steps to improve your life. When you avoid new challenges or experiences, you limit your potential and create a self-imposed barrier to growth. This can lead to a stagnant mindset where you believe change is impossible or too risky, further entrenching feelings of powerlessness.

The relationship between comfort zones and the fear of change is a crucial factor to consider. People often resist leaving their comfort zones because they fear the unknown, which can trigger anxiety and discomfort. This resistance to change can prevent you from exploring new opportunities, learning new skills, and ultimately realizing your full potential. Understanding that the comfort zone is a place of psychological safety but never a place of growth is the first step toward overcoming this resistance and embracing the opportunities that lie beyond it.

Benefits of Leaving Your Comfort Zone

Stepping out of your comfort zone is essential for both personal and professional growth. When you challenge yourself to move beyond familiar boundaries, you open the door to new experiences that can enhance your skills, broaden your perspectives, and increase your confidence. Growth rarely happens in a state of comfort; it occurs when you push yourself to face new challenges and overcome obstacles.

TIP: Realizing that your comfort zone is a place of safety but never a place of growth is the first step toward seeing opportunities that lie beyond it.

One of the key benefits of leaving the comfort zone is the development of resilience. Exposing yourself to new situations and challenges teaches you to adapt to changing circumstances and recover from setbacks more effectively. This resilience is beneficial in overcoming immediate challenges and strengthens your ability to handle future obstacles with greater confidence and composure.

Discomfort, while often perceived negatively, plays a vital role in building adaptability and confidence. By embracing discomfort and learning to navigate it, you develop the mental and emotional flexibility needed to thrive in unfamiliar environments. By persevering through the discomfort and learning as you go, you not only complete the immediate task but also expand your skill set and gain confidence to tackle more challenging tasks in the future.

Real personal and professional growth occurs beyond your comfort zone, where you must take calculated risks and push your boundaries. Examples of this might include learning a new language, starting a new job, or traveling to an unfamiliar place. Each of these experiences involves stepping into the unknown, but they also offer immense opportunities for personal development. By taking risks, you expand your comfort zone and become more capable and confident in your abilities.

How to Expand Your Comfort Zone

Expanding your comfort zone doesn't have to be overwhelming; it can be achieved gradually through a series of small, manageable steps. One effective technique is setting small, achievable challenges that push you slightly beyond your comfort level.

For example, if public speaking is something you find intimidating (as do most people), start by speaking in front of a small group of friends or colleagues. When you become more comfortable, you can gradually increase the size of your audience or the complexity of your presentations. Over time, what was once outside your comfort zone becomes a new area of competence.

Trying new experiences, such as taking up a new hobby, attending a social event where you don't know anyone, or tackling a difficult task at work, can also help push your boundaries and encourage personal growth — thus expanding your comfort zone. These activities force you to confront uncertainty and develop the skills to manage it effectively.

Embracing uncertainty is another powerful way to expand your comfort zone. Life is inherently unpredictable, and learning to navigate it with a mindset of curiosity rather than fear can open up new possibilities for growth.

Instead of avoiding unclear or undefined situations, approach them as opportunities to learn and grow. This shift in mindset helps you become more adaptable and open to change, which is essential for continuous personal development.

Cultivating a mindset of curiosity and openness to change is key to expanding your comfort zone and achieving long-term growth. Curiosity drives you to explore new ideas, ask better questions, and seek out experiences that challenge your existing beliefs and assumptions. By developing curiosity, you make stepping out of your comfort zone easier because you are motivated by the desire to learn and discover rather than being held back by fear of the unknown.

On the other hand, openness to change involves a willingness to adapt to new circumstances and embrace the opportunities that come with them. This doesn't mean abandoning your values or goals but being flexible in how you achieve them. When you are open to change, you are more likely to see challenges as opportunities for growth rather than threats to your comfort and security.

Stepping out of your comfort zone is essential for personal and professional growth. By understanding the limitations of the comfort zone, recognizing the benefits of discomfort, and employing strategies to expand your boundaries, you can unlock new opportunities and continue evolving in ways that enhance your life and career. Embracing change and growth, even when it's uncomfortable, is a key component of success.

Managing Uncertainty and Change

Uncertainty and change are constants in life, yet they are often sources of anxiety and resistance. However, learning to embrace these inevitable aspects of life is crucial for personal growth. When you approach uncertainty with an open mind and a willingness to adapt, you transform potential obstacles into opportunities for innovation and development.

Here, we'll discuss some benefits of embracing uncertainty and change, and how doing so can lead to greater resilience, creativity, and fulfillment. By shifting your perspective and developing strategies to navigate the unknown, you can turn challenges into catalysts for growth.

The Nature of Change and Uncertainty

Change and uncertainty are intrinsic to life. No matter how carefully we plan or how much we strive for stability, change is inevitable, and uncertainty is always present. Understanding this reality is crucial for developing a mindset that can effectively navigate life's challenges.

Change takes many forms—personal transitions, career shifts, or unexpected life events—and each brings its own set of uncertainties. While seeking security and predictability is natural, resisting change can perpetuate a victim mentality, where you feel powerless and controlled by external circumstances.

Resistance to change often stems from fear—fear of the unknown, fear of losing control, or fear of failure. This resistance can manifest as anxiety, stress, or a desire to cling to familiar routines, even when they no longer serve you. The psychological impact of change can be significant, leading to feelings of instability and vulnerability.

However, adaptability—the ability to adjust your thoughts, behaviors, and emotions in response to change—is a vital skill that can mitigate these negative effects. By embracing adaptability, you can approach change with resilience and confidence, transforming uncertainty into a manageable and positive force.

Reframing Change as Opportunity

To thrive in the face of change, it's essential to reframe it as an opportunity rather than a threat. This shift in perspective can fundamentally alter how you experience and respond to change. Instead of viewing change with apprehension, learn to see it as a chance to grow, learn, and explore new possibilities.

One technique for reframing change is to focus on the potential benefits rather than the perceived risks. Ask yourself, *"What opportunities might this change bring?"* or *"How can I use this situation to my advantage?"* or even, *"How will I grow by adapting to this change?"* By redirecting your attention to the positive aspects, you reduce the fear-based reaction and adopt a more proactive stance. This approach lessens anxiety and empowers you to take control of your circumstances, turning change into a stepping stone for personal and professional development.

Strategies for Navigating Change

Navigating change effectively requires practical strategies that help you stay grounded, maintain a positive outlook, and adapt to new circumstances. One of the first steps in managing change is to focus on staying grounded. This can involve practices like mindfulness or meditation, which help you remain present and calm in the midst of uncertainty. By grounding yourself, you create a stable internal environment that can withstand external fluctuations.

Maintaining a positive outlook is another critical strategy. While change can be challenging, focusing on the potential for growth and improvement can help you stay motivated and optimistic. Surrounding yourself with a supportive network that encourages your efforts can also make a significant difference. Whether through friends, family, or professional networks, seeking support ensures that you have a safety net to rely on during times of transition.

Developing flexibility and adaptability are key skills for thriving in an ever-changing environment. Flexibility allows you to adjust your plans and expectations as circumstances evolve, while adaptability enables you to learn and grow in response to new challenges. These skills are particularly important in our modern world, where change is constant, fast, and unpredictable. By cultivating these abilities, you can navigate change with greater ease and confidence, turning challenges into opportunities for success.

Finally, continuous learning and self-improvement are essential to staying ahead of changes and embracing new possibilities. In a constantly evolving society, committing to lifelong learning ensures that you remain relevant and prepared for whatever comes your way. This might involve acquiring new skills, staying informed about industry trends, or pursuing personal development goals. By embracing a mindset of growth and learning, you not only adapt to change but also position yourself to capitalize on the opportunities it presents.

Embracing uncertainty and change is not about eliminating fear or discomfort but about developing the skills and mindset necessary to navigate these inevitable aspects of life. By reframing change as an opportunity, adopting practical strategies for managing transitions, and committing to continuous growth, you can transform uncertainty into a powerful tool for development.

Setting Goals and Pursuing Dreams

Setting goals and pursuing your dreams are fundamental steps in creating a fulfilling and purpose-driven life. Goals give you direction and clarity, transforming vague aspirations into actionable plans, while the pursuit of your dreams fuels motivation and passion. In this section, we will examine the importance of setting meaningful goals that align with your values and aspirations, and how to create a roadmap to achieve them. By understanding the connection between goal-setting and personal growth, you can take deliberate steps toward realizing your dreams, no matter how ambitious they may be.

The Importance of Goal Setting in Personal Growth

Goal setting is a powerful tool for personal growth and transformation. It plays a critical role in breaking free from the victim mentality by shifting your focus from what you can't control to what you can achieve. When you set clear, intentional goals, you begin to take control of your life's direction, moving from a passive to an active stance. This shift helps you realize you have the agency to shape your future.

Achieving goals, no matter how small, builds confidence and reinforces the belief that you can succeed. Each accomplishment boosts your motivation, creating a positive feedback loop that encourages you to set and pursue even more ambitious goals.

Moreover, goal setting provides a sense of purpose by giving you something meaningful to strive for. It helps you align your daily actions with your long-term vision, ensuring that you're not just going through the motions but actively working toward something that matters to you.

The connection between goal setting and long-term growth is deep. Consistently setting and achieving goals lays the foundation for sustained personal and professional development. Goals act as milestones on your journey, marking your progress and helping you stay focused on your broader aspirations. Over time, this disciplined approach to goal setting can lead to significant growth, both in your career and in your personal life.

Creating Effective and Meaningful Goals

Setting effective and meaningful goals requires more than just deciding what you want to achieve. It involves a thoughtful process of planning and alignment with your core values and long-term aspirations. One of the most effective frameworks for goal setting is the SMART criteria, which stands for Specific, Measurable, Achievable, Relevant, and Time-bound.

- *Specific:* Clearly define what you want to accomplish. The more specific your goal, the easier it is to focus your efforts.

- *Measurable:* Establish criteria for tracking your progress and determining when you've achieved your goal.

- *Achievable:* Ensure that your goal is realistic, given your current resources and constraints.

- *Relevant:* Align your goal with your broader life objectives and values, ensuring it's something that truly matters to you.

- **Time-bound**: Set a deadline to create a sense of urgency and prevent procrastination.

Aligning your goals with your values, strengths, and aspirations is crucial for maintaining motivation. When your goals resonate with what you truly care about, you're more likely to stay committed, even when challenges arise. It's also important to break down larger, long-term goals into smaller, actionable steps. This approach makes daunting tasks more manageable and allows you to celebrate incremental progress, keeping you motivated and on track.

Example of Using SMART Goals

To illustrate how SMART goals can be effectively applied, let's explore an example in the context of career development. Imagine you have a dream of becoming a project manager within your company, but currently, you're in a more junior role. Here's how you could set a SMART goal to help you achieve this goal:

Specific

Instead of setting a vague goal like *"I want to advance in my career,"* make it specific. For example, *"I want to be promoted to a project manager position within my company."*

Measurable

Determine how you will measure your progress toward this goal. For example, you might decide to measure progress by completing a relevant certification, gaining experience by leading smaller projects, and receiving positive feedback from your supervisors.

A measurable goal could be, *"I will complete a Project Management Professional (PMP) certification and successfully manage three smaller projects within the next year."*

Achievable

Consider whether your goal is realistic and attainable, given your current circumstances. If becoming a project manager within a year is feasible with the resources and time you have, then it's achievable.

Ensure that your goal challenges you, but is not so far out of reach that it becomes discouraging. For example, *"I will dedicate 5-7 hours per week to studying for the PMP exam while managing smaller projects to build my experience."*

Relevant

Make sure your goal aligns with your broader career aspirations and values. If you're passionate about leadership and project management, and if this goal fits into your long-term career plan, it's relevant.

For instance, *"Achieving this goal is aligned with my long-term career objective of becoming a senior project manager and eventually leading a department."*

Time-bound

Set a clear deadline for achieving your goal. This helps create a sense of urgency and keeps you focused. A time-bound goal could be, *"I will achieve my promotion to project manager within 18 months by completing the PMP certification within the next 12 months and gaining hands-on experience by the end of the following six months."*

Putting it all Together

Here's what your completed SMART goal might look like after combining all of the elements:

"I want to be promoted to a project manager position within my company. To achieve this, I will complete the PMP certification within the next 12 months and successfully manage three smaller projects to gain the necessary experience. I will dedicate 5-7 hours per week to studying for the certification and apply the skills I learn to these projects. My goal is to secure a promotion within the next 18 months, aligning with my long-term career aspiration of becoming a senior project manager."

Breaking Down the Goal:

- **Specific:** Aiming for a project manager position.

- **Measurable:** Completing the PMP certification and managing three smaller projects.

- **Achievable:** Dedicating a realistic amount of time to study and gain experience.

- **Relevant:** Aligns with long-term career aspirations.

- **Time-bound:** Setting a clear deadline of 18 months.

By applying the SMART framework, you turn your broader dream of career advancement into a clear, actionable plan. This not only increases your chances of success but also provides you with a structured approach to tracking your progress, adjusting your efforts, and staying motivated along the way. Using SMART goals helps ensure that each step you take brings you closer to realizing your dream.

In the next chapter, we'll tackle the essential aspects of building healthy relationships by communicating assertively, setting and maintaining healthy boundaries, and nurturing supportive connections. These components are crucial for breaking free from the victim mentality and fostering relationships that contribute to personal empowerment and growth

Chapter 9
Building Healthy Relationships

"Know your worth and please don't invest in toxic people or relationships, because any bond that requires servicing is not worth your time."

— Masaba Gupta

ALRIGHT. WE'VE COME TO an inflection point in our journey and, arguably, the most important chapter in the book.

Why? . . .

Because it is nearly impossible to break free from a victim mentality when you surround yourself with people who refuse to do the same. In fact, it is commonly stated that *"you are a composite image of your five closest friends."* This powerful statement recognizes that healthy relationships are the cornerstone of a fulfilling life.

In this chapter, we will explore the essential elements of creating and nurturing relationships that are supportive, respectful, and mutually beneficial. By understanding the principles of effective communication, setting healthy boundaries, building connections based on trust and empathy, and letting go of toxic relationships, you can enhance the quality of your life.

Communicating Assertively

Effective communication is the foundation of any healthy relationship, and assertiveness is a key component of that communication. Assertive communication allows you to express your thoughts, feelings, and needs clearly and respectfully, without compromising the rights of others. It strikes a balance between passive communication, where you might withhold your true feelings, and aggressive communication, where your needs might overshadow those of others.

In this section, you'll learn the importance of assertiveness in building strong, healthy relationships and how it can help you maintain your boundaries while fostering mutual respect and understanding. By mastering assertive communication skills, you can enhance your interactions, reduce misunderstandings, and create more positive and effective connections with those around you.

What is Assertive Communication?

Assertive communication is the ability to express your thoughts, feelings, and needs openly and honestly while also respecting the rights of others. This balanced communication style differs significantly from passive, aggressive, and passive-aggressive approaches.

- *Passive communication* involves holding back your true thoughts and feelings, often to avoid conflict or because of a lack of confidence. This can lead to frustration, resentment, and feeling overlooked or undervalued.

- *Aggressive communication* is characterized by dominating others to get your way, often at the expense of their feelings or needs. This approach can damage relationships and create an environment of fear or hostility.

- *Passive-aggressive communication* combines elements of both passive and aggressive styles. In this style, a person might express their dissatisfaction indirectly or through sarcasm, leading to confusion and unresolved issues.

In contrast, assertive communication allows you to stand up for yourself and express your needs clearly and respectfully, fostering healthier relationships and enhancing self-respect. Assertiveness is particularly empowering because it supports the shift from a victim mentality to an empowered mindset. By communicating assertively, you take ownership of your needs and feelings rather than feeling helpless or dependent on others to understand you without clear communication.

Elements of Assertive Communication

Assertive communication is built on clear, direct, and respectful exchanges. The key to assertiveness is expressing your needs and desires without diminishing the other person's feelings or rights. This involves several crucial elements:

Clarity and Directness: Speak clearly and directly about what you need or how you feel, without *'beating around the bush'* or being overly vague. This helps prevent misunderstandings and ensures that your message is understood as intended.

Respectful Expression: While being direct, it's equally important to remain respectful. Assertiveness is not about overpowering others; it's about ensuring that your voice is heard in a way that respects both your rights and those of others. This involves using calm, non-threatening language using a firm yet polite tone.

Expressing Boundaries: Assertive communication involves clearly stating your boundaries—what you are and are not comfortable with—without feeling guilty or hostile. It's about expressing your limits in a way that others can understand and respect, helping to prevent overcommitment or burnout.

Active Listening: An essential part of assertive communication is active listening. This means fully engaging with what the other person is saying, validating their feelings, and acknowledging their perspective, even as you maintain your stance. Active listening helps create a balanced dialogue where both parties feel heard and respected.

Practical Strategies for Practicing Assertiveness

Developing assertiveness is a skill that can be honed through practice. Here are some practical strategies to help you become more assertive in your communication:

Use "I" Statements: One of the most effective techniques for assertive communication is using *"I"* statements, such as *"I feel ..." "I need..."* or *"I would like..."* This approach focuses on your experience rather than placing blame or making accusations, which can help prevent the other person from becoming defensive.

Maintain Eye Contact: Eye contact is a powerful nonverbal cue that conveys confidence and sincerity. Maintaining eye contact while speaking helps to reinforce your message and shows that you are engaged and serious about what you're saying.

Assertive Body Language: Your body language is crucial in how your message is received. Stand or sit up straight, keep your posture open, and use gestures that reinforce your words. Avoid crossing your arms or fidgeting, as these can undermine your message and make you appear less confident.

Handle Difficult Conversations with Confidence: When facing challenging conversations or conflicts, it is important to stay calm and focused on the issue. Prepare yourself by thinking through what you want to say and how you will respond to potential pushback. Remember to stick to your points without becoming aggressive or defensive.

Practice Regularly: Like any skill, assertiveness improves with regular practice. Start by incorporating assertive communication into less intimidating situations, such as everyday conversations with friends or colleagues. As you become more comfortable, gradually apply these techniques to more challenging scenarios in your personal and professional life.

By consistently practicing these strategies, you'll build the confidence and skills necessary to communicate assertively in various environments. Over time, this will lead to stronger, more positive relationships and greater empowerment in your interactions with others.

Setting Healthy Boundaries

Setting healthy boundaries is essential for maintaining balanced and respectful relationships. Boundaries define what is acceptable and unacceptable in your interactions with others, ensuring that your needs, values, and limits are respected. Without clear boundaries, you may find yourself overcommitted, stressed, or resentful, which can strain your relationships and harm your well-being.

In this section, we will discuss establishing and maintaining healthy boundaries in both personal and professional contexts.

By understanding how to communicate your boundaries effectively and assertively, you can protect your emotional and mental health.

The Importance of Relationship Boundaries

Personal boundaries are the physical, emotional, and mental limits you set to protect yourself from being manipulated, used, or violated by others. They define whether behaviors are acceptable, creating a framework for healthy, respectful interactions. Boundaries maintain balance and mutual respect, whether they are personal, professional, or social.

Setting boundaries also helps prevent codependency, where one person becomes overly reliant on another for their emotional needs. Without boundaries, you may take on too much responsibility for others' happiness or well-being, leading to resentment and burnout. Clear boundaries let you prioritize your needs and well-being, ensuring you do not overextend yourself or compromise your values.

When you set and enforce boundaries, you take control of your interactions and relationships, reducing the likelihood of being taken advantage of or feeling powerless. Boundaries help you assert your needs and limits confidently, reinforcing your self-respect and helping you maintain a sense of autonomy.

Identifying and Establishing Boundaries

The first step in setting healthy boundaries is identifying your personal limits—what you are comfortable with and what you are not. This involves self-reflection and an honest assessment of your needs, values, and emotional triggers. Consider areas in your life where you feel overwhelmed, taken for granted, or uncomfortable, as these are often indicators of where boundaries may be lacking.

Once you have identified the areas where boundaries are needed, the next step is to communicate them clearly to others. This can be challenging, especially if you fear conflict or rejection, but it is essential for maintaining healthy relationships. When expressing your boundaries, be direct and specific about what you need, and do so in a calm and respectful manner. For example, if you need time to yourself after a busy day, you might say, *"I need some quiet time after work to recharge. Can we schedule our conversation for later in the evening?"*

It's important to understand that setting boundaries is not a one-time event but an ongoing process. As your relationships and circumstances change over time, so too may your boundaries. Regularly reflecting on your needs and adjusting your boundaries accordingly ensures that they remain relevant and effective. This ongoing process requires self-awareness and a willingness to advocate for yourself, even when it's uncomfortable.

Maintaining and Enforcing Boundaries

Maintaining and enforcing boundaries is essential for making sure that others respect you. Consistency is key—if you allow your boundaries to be crossed without addressing them, you send the message that they are unimportant or can be ignored. When someone violates your boundaries, it's essential to address the issue calmly and assertively, reiterating your limits and the importance of respecting them.

Dealing with pushback is a common challenge when enforcing boundaries. Some people may react negatively when you establish limits, especially if they are used to overstepping them. It's important to stay firm and not allow guilt or fear of conflict to weaken your resolve. Remember that maintaining your boundaries is a form of self-respect and self-care. It's about protecting your well-being and ensuring your relationships are based on mutual respect.

As your relationships and life circumstances change, your boundaries may need to be reassessed and adjusted. For example, a boundary that was once necessary for a certain relationship may no longer be relevant as the relationship or circumstances evolve. Regularly checking in with yourself and your boundaries allows you to make adjustments as needed, ensuring they continue serving your best interests.

> **TIP:** Remember that maintaining your boundaries is a form of self-respect and self-care.

Setting, maintaining, and enforcing healthy boundaries is essential for creating balanced, respectful relationships and protecting your overall well-being. By understanding the importance of boundaries, identifying where they are needed, and developing strategies to uphold them, you can build stronger, more fulfilling relationships.

Step-by-Step Guide for Setting Boundaries

Setting healthy boundaries is essential for maintaining balance, respect, and well-being in your relationships. This step-by-step guide will help you identify, establish, and maintain effective boundaries.

Step 1: Self-Reflection and Awareness

Identify Your Needs and Values: Begin by reflecting on your core values and needs. What is most important to you in your relationships? What do you need to feel respected, safe, and valued? Understanding these needs will help you determine where boundaries are necessary.

Recognize Boundary Violations: Consider situations where you've felt uncomfortable, stressed, or resentful. These feelings often indicate that a boundary has been crossed or is lacking. Consider specific instances in your personal and professional life where you wish things had gone differently.

Understand Your Emotional Triggers: Identify any emotional triggers that cause you to feel overwhelmed or upset. Knowing your triggers will help you recognize when a boundary needs to be set to protect your emotional well-being.

Step 2: Define Your Boundaries

Determine Specific Boundaries: Based on your reflections, define specific boundaries that align with your needs and values. These could be related to time, energy, personal space, emotional involvement, or any other aspect of your life that requires protection.

Prioritize Your Boundaries: Not all boundaries are equally urgent. Prioritize them based on how much they impact your well-being and relationships. Start with the boundaries that address your most pressing needs.

Consider Flexibility: While some boundaries may be non-negotiable, others might require flexibility depending on the situation. Decide which boundaries are firm and which can be adjusted if necessary.

Step 3: Plan Your Communication

Prepare Your Message: Plan how you will communicate your boundaries clearly and assertively. Use "I" statements to express your needs without blaming or accusing others. For example, *"I need time alone after work to unwind, so I would appreciate it if we could talk later in the evening."*

Anticipate Reactions: Consider how the other person might react to your boundary-setting. Prepare yourself for possible pushback or discomfort, and think about how you will respond calmly and assertively.

Choose the Right Time and Place: Plan to communicate your boundaries in a setting where both parties can have a calm, open and respectful conversation. Avoid bringing up boundaries during moments of tension or conflict.

Step 4: Set and Communicate Your Boundaries

Start the Conversation: Approach the conversation with confidence and clarity. Clearly state your boundary and the reasons behind it. Be respectful but firm in your communication, ensuring that the other person understands your needs.

Stay Calm and Assertive: Maintain a calm and assertive tone throughout the conversation. Avoid apologizing excessively or backing down if you face resistance. Remember that your boundaries are important for your well-being.

Be Open to Dialogue: While it's important to be firm, also be open to discussing your boundaries and addressing any concerns the other person may have. This can help promote mutual understanding and respect.

Step 5: Enforce and Maintain Your Boundaries

Be Consistent: Consistency is key to maintaining boundaries. If someone crosses your boundary, address it immediately and remind them of your limits. Consistently enforcing your boundaries reinforces their importance.

Handle Pushback Assertively: If someone reacts negatively to your boundary, respond assertively without compromising your needs. Reiterate the importance of the boundary and why it's necessary for your well-being.

Practice Self-Care: Setting and maintaining boundaries can be challenging, especially if you're not used to it. Engage in self-care activities that help you recharge and stay centered. This will support your emotional and mental health as you navigate boundary-setting.

Step 6: Reevaluate and Adjust as Needed

Regularly Reflect on Your Boundaries: Periodically assess how your boundaries are working. Are they being respected?

Do they still align with your needs and values? Reflection helps you stay aware of any necessary changes.

Adjust Boundaries as Relationships Evolve: Relationships change over time, and your boundaries may need to evolve as well. Be open to adjusting your boundaries as needed to reflect changes in your life or relationships.

Seek Support if Necessary: If you're struggling to maintain boundaries, consider seeking support from a trusted friend, mentor, or therapist. They can offer guidance and encouragement as you navigate challenging situations.

Step 7: Celebrate Your Progress

Acknowledge Your Efforts: Recognize the effort you've put into setting and maintaining your boundaries. It's an important step toward self-empowerment and healthier relationships.

Celebrate Your Successes: Whether small or large, celebrate your success in setting boundaries. Each step forward is a positive move toward a more balanced and fulfilling life.

By following these steps, you can effectively set and maintain healthy boundaries that protect your well-being and enhance your relationships. Remember, boundary-setting is an ongoing process that requires patience, practice, and perseverance.

Nurturing Supportive Connections

Building and maintaining supportive connections is vital for your emotional well-being and personal growth. These relationships provide the encouragement, understanding, and trust needed to navigate life's challenges and celebrate its joys. Whether with friends, family, colleagues, or mentors, supportive connections form the foundation of a strong social network that empowers you to thrive. Here, we'll explore the importance of nurturing these connections, the qualities that make a relationship truly supportive, and strategies for fostering deeper, more meaningful bonds with the people who matter most.

The Value of Supportive Relationships

Supportive relationships provide the emotional foundation that helps you navigate challenges, celebrate successes, and continue your journey toward empowerment. Supportive relationships are characterized by mutual respect, trust, and encouragement, which create a safe environment where you feel valued and understood.

When you have people in your life who truly support you, you are more likely to feel confident, secure, and motivated. These connections help reduce stress, anxiety, and feelings of isolation by providing a sense of belonging and reassurance. Moreover, supportive relationships encourage you to pursue your goals and dreams, knowing that you have a network of people who believe in your potential.

Building a Supportive Network

Cultivating and maintaining supportive relationships requires intentional effort. One effective technique is to surround yourself with individuals who inspire you, share your values, and encourage your growth. Shared activities, such as hobbies, community events, or professional groups, can help strengthen these bonds and create a sense of camaraderie.

Reciprocity is a key element of healthy relationships. Giving and receiving support is important, creating a balanced dynamic where both parties feel valued and appreciated. Being there for others in times of need, offering a listening ear, or providing encouragement can strengthen your connections and foster deeper, more meaningful relationships.

Expanding your network with like-minded, positive individuals can also enhance your supportive connections. Proactively engaging with new people who share your interests or values can lead to the development of enriching relationships. Whether through social events, networking opportunities, or online communities, connecting with others can broaden your support system and introduce you to new perspectives and opportunities.

Identifying and Severing Toxic Relationships

Toxic people and relationships are those that consistently bring negativity, stress, and harm into your life. These relationships can be draining, demoralizing, and damaging to your mental and emotional well-being. Toxic individuals often exhibit behaviors such as manipulation, control, criticism, and lack of empathy. Over time, these behaviors can erode your self-esteem, create anxiety, and perpetuate a cycle of negativity that hinders your personal growth and happiness.

It's important to recognize that toxic relationships can exist in various forms—whether with friends, family members, romantic partners, or colleagues. The toxicity might not always be blatantly obvious; it can be subtle and insidious, gradually wearing you down mentally and emotionally. Identifying these relationships early on is crucial for protecting your mental health and well-being.

Signs of Toxic People and Relationships

Here are some key signs to help you identify toxic people and relationships:

Constant Criticism and Blame: Toxic individuals criticize you excessively, making you feel inadequate or incapable. They may also blame you for their own mistakes or problems, refusing to take responsibility for their actions.

Manipulation and Control: Toxic people often manipulate others to get their way. This can involve guilt-tripping, lying, or using emotional blackmail to control your actions and decisions. They may also try to isolate you from other supportive relationships to maintain control.

Lack of Empathy: A lack of empathy is a hallmark of toxic behavior. Toxic individuals may dismiss or minimize your feelings, showing little concern for your well-being. They may also be indifferent to how their actions affect you or others.

Frequent Drama and Conflict: Toxic relationships are marked by constant drama, conflict, and emotional turmoil. These individuals thrive on chaos and may create unnecessary problems or arguments to maintain a sense of control or self-importance.

Jealousy and Insecurity: Toxic people may be excessively jealous or insecure, leading them to undermine your success or happiness. They may try to sabotage your achievements or create competition where none exists.

Lack of Support and Encouragement: In a healthy relationship, both parties support and encourage each other's growth and happiness. Toxic individuals may withhold support, belittle your goals, or make you feel guilty for pursuing your dreams.

Boundary Violations: Toxic people often disregard your boundaries, whether emotional, physical, or mental. They may push you to do things you're uncomfortable with, ignore your requests, or invade your personal space.

The Importance of Severing Toxic Ties

Severing ties with toxic people and relationships is essential for preserving your mental health and emotional well-being. Remaining in these relationships can lead to long-term psychological damage, including chronic stress, anxiety, depression, and a diminished sense of self-worth. Here's why it's so important to remove toxic influences from your life:

Protecting Your Self-Esteem: Toxic relationships often chip away at your self-esteem, making you doubt your abilities and worth. By distancing yourself from toxic individuals, you can begin to rebuild your confidence and self-respect.

Reducing Stress and Anxiety: Constant exposure to toxic behavior can lead to chronic stress and anxiety. Severing these ties allows you to create a more peaceful and stable environment, reducing the emotional turmoil that toxic relationships cause.

Fostering Personal Growth: Toxic relationships can stunt personal growth by keeping you in a cycle of negativity and self-doubt. Removing these influences opens up space for positive relationships and experiences that encourage development and well-being.

Regaining Control of Your Life: Toxic individuals often seek to control or manipulate those around them. By ending these relationships, you reclaim control over your life, decisions, and happiness.

Encouraging Healthy Relationships: Letting go of toxic people makes room for healthier, more supportive relationships. Surrounding yourself with positive influences strengthens your resilience, boosts your mood, and enhances your overall quality of life.

Preserving Your Mental and Emotional Health: The longer you stay in a toxic relationship, the more harm it can do to your mental and emotional health. Severing these ties is crucial to healing and creating a life where you feel valued, respected, and empowered.

How to Sever Ties with Toxic People

Ending a toxic relationship can be challenging, especially if the person is someone you care about or are closely connected to. However, it's essential to prioritize your mental health and well-being. Here are some steps to take:

1. ***Acknowledge the Problem:*** The first step is to recognize that the relationship is toxic and negatively affecting your life. Acknowledging the issue is essential for moving forward.

2. ***Set Firm Boundaries:*** Before cutting ties completely, you may want to set firm boundaries with the toxic

individual. Clearly communicate your limits and expectations, and be prepared to enforce them.

3. *Distance Yourself:* Gradually distancing yourself from the toxic person can help ease the transition. Reduce the time you spend with them, limit communication, and avoid situations where they can exert influence over you.

4. *Seek Support:* Ending a toxic relationship can be emotionally taxing. Seek support from trusted friends, family members, or a licensed therapist who can provide guidance and encouragement during this process.

5. *Cut Ties if Necessary:* In some cases, it may be necessary to cut ties completely, especially if the toxic person refuses to respect your boundaries or continues to harm you. This may involve ending all communication and removing them from your social circles.

6. *Focus on Self-Care:* After severing ties with a toxic person, prioritize self-care and healing. Engage in activities that bring you joy, practice mindfulness, and surround yourself with positive influences.

Identifying and severing ties with toxic people is essential for protecting your mental health and fostering a life of empowerment and growth. While it may be difficult, removing toxic influences from your life allows you to create room for healthier relationships that support your well-being and personal development.

Let's move on to the next chapter, where we'll focus on the practices of gratitude and mindfulness as key strategies for overcoming the victim mentality and cultivating a joyful, fulfilling life.

Chapter 10

Practicing Gratitude, Mindfulness and Joy

"Gratitude makes sense of our past, brings peace for today, and creates a vision for tomorrow."
— Melody Beattie

I T'S EASY TO GET caught up in the stresses and demands of day-to-day life, often losing sight of the positive aspects of our lives that surround us. Practicing gratitude and mindfulness offers a powerful way to reconnect with the present moment, appreciate what we have, and cultivate a sense of inner peace and fulfillment.

These practices are not just about feeling good—they're about developing a mindset that breeds resilience, improves mental health, and enhances overall well-being. In this chapter, we will discuss the profound benefits of gratitude and mindfulness and how incorporating these practices into your daily life can transform your perspective, strengthen your relationships, and lead to a more balanced and joyful existence.

Cultivating Gratitude in Daily Life

Gratitude is more than just a passing feeling of thankfulness—it's a powerful mindset that can transform how you experience the world. Focusing on the positives in your life, even amidst challenges, can shift your perspective from one of lack to one of abundance.

Cultivating gratitude in your daily life helps you appreciate the small joys, deepen your connections with others, and foster a sense of contentment and inner peace that transcends external circumstances. Let's discover practical ways to integrate gratitude into your everyday routine, from simple exercises to mindful reflections.

The Power of Gratitude

Gratitude is the practice of recognizing and appreciating the positive aspects of your life, no matter how small or seemingly insignificant. It's more than a momentary feeling; it's a mindset that can have profound psychological benefits. When you practice gratitude, you shift your focus from what is lacking in your life to what is abundant. This change in perspective helps to foster a sense of contentment and fulfillment, even in the face of challenges.

Gratitude plays a crucial role in overcoming the victim mentality. When you regularly acknowledge the good in your life, you move away from a mindset of helplessness and toward one of empowerment. Instead of constantly dwelling on what's wrong, gratitude helps you to see what's right, providing a foundation for resilience and a more positive outlook on life.

Techniques for Practicing Gratitude

There are several techniques for incorporating gratitude into your daily routine, each offering a unique way to cultivate this powerful mindset. Here are just a few:

Daily Gratitude Journaling: One of the most popular methods is keeping a gratitude journal. Each day, take a few moments to write down three to five things you are thankful for. These can range from significant events to small, everyday moments that brought you joy. Over time, this practice trains your mind to notice and appreciate the positive aspects of your life.

Gratitude Meditation: Incorporating gratitude into your meditation practice can deepen your sense of appreciation. During your mindfulness exercises, focus on feelings of gratitude—whether for your health, loved ones, or simple pleasures. This practice not only enhances your meditation but also reinforces a positive mindset throughout the day.

Expressing Gratitude in Interactions: Another powerful way to practice gratitude is by regularly expressing appreciation to those around you. Whether it's thanking a colleague for their help, expressing love to a family member, or acknowledging a friend's support, these interactions strengthen your relationships and foster a culture of gratitude in your social circles.

The Impact of Gratitude on Mindset

Consistently practicing gratitude can significantly impact your overall mindset and well-being. By focusing on what you have rather than what you lack, gratitude fosters a positive outlook that can enhance your resilience. This positive perspective makes it easier to navigate life's challenges, as you are more inclined to see obstacles as opportunities rather than insurmountable problems.

Gratitude also helps reduce stress, anxiety, and feelings of helplessness. When you focus on the positives, your mind is less likely to dwell on negative thoughts, which can help reduce the emotional burden of stress and anxiety. Over time, a habit of gratitude can lead to sustained improvements in mental and emotional well-being, helping you maintain a balanced and optimistic approach to life.

Practicing Mindfulness to Stay Present

As you go through life, it's easy to become consumed by worries about the future or regrets about the past, often losing touch with the present moment. Practicing mindfulness offers a powerful way to anchor yourself in the here and now, fostering a deeper connection with your thoughts, emotions, and surroundings.

Mindfulness is the practice of paying full attention to the present moment without judgment. It allows you to experience life more fully and reduce stress and anxiety. In this section, we'll look at the principles of mindfulness and how you can integrate this practice into your daily routine. By staying present through mindfulness, you can enhance your awareness, improve your emotional well-being, and cultivate a more balanced and peaceful life.

The Importance of Mindfulness

Mindfulness is the practice of fully engaging with the present moment, bringing your attention to what is happening right now without judgment or distraction. This approach to living offers numerous benefits for mental and emotional well-being. By focusing on the present, mindfulness helps you break free from the cycle of negative thinking that often accompanies the victim mentality. Instead of being consumed by past regrets or future anxieties, mindfulness encourages you to experience life as it unfolds, creating a sense of inner peace and acceptance.

Mindfulness also plays a crucial role in increasing self-awareness. By paying close attention to your thoughts, feelings, and bodily sensations, you gain a deeper understanding of your emotional responses and behavioral patterns. This heightened awareness allows for better emotional regulation, enabling you to respond to situations with clarity and calmness rather than reacting impulsively or out of habit.

Mindfulness Techniques

There are several mindfulness techniques that you can incorporate into your daily life to help you stay present and grounded. These practices are simple but effective tools for reducing stress, improving focus, and enhancing overall well-being.

Guided Breathing Exercises: Focusing on your breath is one of the most fundamental mindfulness practices. By taking slow, deep breaths and concentrating on the sensation of the air entering and leaving your body, you can anchor yourself in the present moment. This practice helps calm the mind, reduce anxiety, and bring your attention back to the here and now whenever your thoughts begin to wander.

Body Scan Meditation: This technique involves mentally scanning your body from head to toe, becoming aware of any physical sensations, tension, or discomfort. By directing your attention to different parts of your body, you can release tension and become more in tune with how your body feels in the present moment. The body scan meditation is a powerful way to ground yourself, especially when you feel disconnected or overwhelmed.

Mindful Observation: Engaging fully with your environment and daily activities is another way to practice mindfulness. Whether you are eating, walking, or simply sitting, take a moment to observe your surroundings with full attention. Notice the colors, sounds, smells, and textures around you. By immersing yourself in these sensory experiences, you can enhance your presence and focus, making even mundane tasks more meaningful and enjoyable.

Integrating Mindfulness into Daily Life

Incorporating mindfulness into your daily routine doesn't require major changes—small, consistent practices can make a significant difference. Here are some tips for bringing mindfulness into your daily life:

Mindful Eating: Instead of rushing through meals, take time to savor each bite. Pay attention to the flavors, textures, and smells of your food. Eating mindfully not only enhances your enjoyment of meals but also helps you develop a healthier relationship with food.

Mindful Walking: Whether you're walking to work, exercising, or simply strolling, turn off distractions and focus on the sensation of walking. Feel the ground beneath your feet, notice the rhythm of your steps, and observe the environment around you. Mindful walking is a simple yet effective way to practice mindfulness and stay connected to the present moment.

Mindful Listening: When engaging in conversations, practice being fully present. Listen without planning your response or letting your mind wander. This type of mindful listening strengthens your connections with others and enhances communication, making interactions more meaningful.

Creating a regular mindfulness practice is key to building consistency and reaping the long-term benefits of staying present. Whether you set aside a few minutes each day for meditation or integrate mindfulness into everyday tasks, the important thing is to practice regularly. Over time, mindfulness can become a natural part of your life, helping you manage stress, anxiety, and emotional triggers more effectively. By using mindfulness as a tool for staying present, you can cultivate a greater sense of peace, clarity, and resilience.

Finding Joy and Fulfillment

In our pursuit of goals and dreams, it's easy to overlook the simple joys and moments of fulfillment that exist in our daily lives. However, true happiness is often found not in grand achievements or future aspirations, but in the present moment—when we allow ourselves to fully experience and appreciate what life has to offer right now.

Finding joy and fulfillment in the moment involves cultivating an awareness of life's small pleasures, nurturing a sense of contentment, and embracing the beauty in everyday experiences. In this section, we'll discuss how to shift your focus from what's missing or what's next to what's here and now. By practicing presence and gratitude, you can discover a deeper sense of happiness and fulfillment that enriches your life on a daily basis.

The Concept of Living in the Present

Living in the present means fully engaging with the current moment, appreciating it for what it is without distraction or judgment. It's about letting go of the past and not worrying about the future. This allows you to experience life as it unfolds, rather than with fear or trepidation about what might happen. This practice is essential for finding joy and fulfillment, shifting your focus from what has been or could be to what is happening right now.

When you dwell on past regrets or future anxieties, you fuel the victim mentality, which keeps you trapped in a cycle of negative thinking and disempowerment. By contrast, living in the present helps you break free from these patterns, encouraging a mindset of acceptance and peace. The connection between mindfulness, presence, and finding joy is profound; by practicing mindfulness, you can stay grounded in the moment and discover the joy that exists in everyday life.

Discovering Fulfillment in Simple Moments

True fulfillment often lies in the simple moments that we too frequently take for granted. By slowing down and taking the time to appreciate these small pleasures, you can cultivate a deeper sense of satisfaction and happiness. Techniques such as savoring your morning coffee, enjoying a walk in nature, or simply noticing the sun's warmth on your skin can help you connect with the joy inherent in these everyday experiences.

Encouraging yourself to slow down and notice the beauty in ordinary moments transforms the mundane into the meaningful. Whether it's the sound of laughter, the taste of a favorite meal, or the comfort of a cozy evening at home, these experiences can bring a profound sense of fulfillment when approached with presence and appreciation. Additionally, being present allows you to deepen your connections with others, making interactions more meaningful and enriching your overall satisfaction.

Cultivating a Joyful Mindset

Joy is not just something that happens to you; it's a choice and a mindset that you can cultivate, even in the face of challenges. Choosing joy means actively seeking out positivity, embracing the good in every situation, and prioritizing your own happiness. This mindset shift can have a transformative impact on your life, helping you to navigate difficulties with grace and optimism.

Practical steps for fostering a joyful mindset include practicing gratitude, staying mindful of the present, and using positive affirmations to reinforce a positive outlook. By regularly reflecting on the things you are grateful for, you train your mind to focus on abundance rather than scarcity. Mindfulness helps you stay grounded in the moment, where joy is most accessible. Positive affirmations, such as *"I choose joy today,"* reinforce your commitment to living a joyful life.

Finally, it's important to prioritize joy and fulfillment as essential components of an empowered life. This means making time for activities that bring you happiness, surrounding yourself with positive influences, and not allowing the pressures of life to overshadow your pursuit of joy. By choosing to live joyfully, you not only enhance your own well-being but also radiate positivity to those around you, creating a ripple effect of happiness and fulfillment in your life and the lives of others.

In the next chapter, we'll discuss how to sustain an empowered lifestyle by creating positive habits, ongoing personal growth, and inspiring others to pursue their own journey of empowerment.

Chapter 11

Living an Empowered Life

"You are today where your thoughts have brought you;
you will be tomorrow where your thoughts take you."
— James Allen

E MPOWERMENT IS NOT A one-time achievement but an
ongoing journey that requires continuous effort and
commitment. After overcoming the victim mentality, setting
boundaries, embracing change, and cultivating mindfulness,
the next challenge is to sustain this empowered mindset. Sustaining empowerment involves developing habits and practices
that reinforce your personal growth, resilience, and self-worth
over the long term.

In this chapter, we'll see how to maintain a sense of empowerment by creating supportive routines, continuous learning,
and inspiring others. By integrating these practices into your
life, you can ensure that the progress you've made thus far is
continually developed and that you're living a life of sustained
fulfillment, confidence, and purpose.

Creating Habits that Support Empowerment

Empowerment is backed up by the daily habits and routines that shape your life. While significant moments of insight and transformation are essential, consistent, everyday actions truly sustain your sense of empowerment. By intentionally creating habits that support your growth, resilience, and self-confidence, you will build a solid foundation that sustains your journey.

In this section, we'll discuss the importance of habit formation in maintaining your empowered mindset and provide practical strategies for developing routines that align with your goals and values. Whether practicing gratitude, setting clear intentions for the day, or engaging in regular self-reflection, these habits will help you stay grounded and continue to thrive.

Why Habits are Important

Habits are the building blocks of your daily life, influencing your behaviors, decisions, and, ultimately, your mindset. Understanding how habits shape behavior is crucial for sustaining empowerment. When you consistently engage in positive, empowering habits, you reinforce a mindset of growth and resilience, making it easier to overcome challenges and maintain a sense of ownership over your life.

The connection between daily habits and long-term personal empowerment cannot be overstated. While major life changes and breakthroughs are important, the small, consistent actions you take daily have the most significant impact on your overall well-being and success. By cultivating habits that align with your goals and values, you create a stable foundation that supports ongoing personal growth.

> *"Your beliefs become your thoughts,*
> *Your thoughts become your words,*
> *Your words become your actions,*
> *Your actions become your habits,*
> *Your habits become your values,*
> *Your values become your destiny."*
> — Mahatma Gandhi

Consistent, positive habits reinforce a shift away from the victim mentality. When you consciously choose habits that empower you—such as setting daily intentions, practicing mindfulness, or engaging in regular self-care—you gradually reshape your mindset to one of empowerment and agency. These habits help you focus on what you can control, rather than dwelling on circumstances that feel overwhelming or beyond your reach.

Identifying Empowering Habits

Before you can implement habits that support your growth, you must know what they are. Start by reflecting on your current routines and behaviors. Are there habits that make you feel stronger, more confident, or more in control? Or are there habits that leave you feeling drained, disempowered, or stuck in a cycle of negativity?

Try journaling, self-reflection, and listening to feedback from trusted friends or mentors. Analyzing your daily routines can pinpoint which habits are serving you and which are not. Once identified, you can focus on building the habits that genuinely enhance your well-being.

Examples of empowering habits include:

- *Daily Goal-Setting:* Starting each day with clear goals helps you stay focused and motivated. Setting achievable, meaningful goals gives you a sense of purpose and direction.

- *Morning Routines:* Establishing a morning routine with activities like exercise, meditation, or reading can set a positive tone for the day and boost your mental and physical energy.

- *Regular Self-Reflection:* Taking time to reflect on your experiences, progress, and challenges allows you to learn from your actions and make informed adjustments to your behavior.

Auditing your habits helps identify which ones align with your goals and which ones need to be adjusted or replaced. This ongoing cycle of reflection and adjustment ensures that your habits remain aligned with your journey toward empowerment.

Maintaining Positive Habits

Building new, empowering habits requires a thoughtful approach. Start by focusing on small, manageable changes rather than trying to overhaul your entire routine at once. For example, if you want to develop a habit of daily exercise, begin with just 10 minutes a day and gradually increase the duration as the habit becomes ingrained. Starting small makes it easier to stay consistent and build momentum.

Consistency is key to habit formation. Sticking to your habits is essential, even when motivation wanes. Techniques such as setting reminders, creating a habit tracker, or linking your new habit to an existing one (a concept known as habit stacking) can help you stay on track.

Celebrating progress is also crucial for maintaining motivation. Acknowledge and reward yourself for sticking to your habits, even in small ways. This positive reinforcement helps to solidify the habit and makes it more enjoyable to continue.

Overcoming obstacles to habit formation, such as procrastination and lack of motivation, requires persistence and self-compassion. Recognize that setbacks are a natural part of the process; don't be too hard on yourself if you have setbacks. Instead, focus on getting back on track as soon as possible and remind yourself of your new habit's benefits.

Maintaining habits over time involves tracking your progress and staying accountable. Regularly reviewing your habits allows you to see how far you've come and make any necessary adjustments. Staying accountable can be achieved by sharing your goals with a friend, finding an accountability partner, joining a supportive community, or using habit-tracking apps.

By intentionally creating and maintaining habits that support empowerment, you can build a life that is aligned with your goals and values. These habits reinforce your sense of empowerment and provide the structure and consistency needed for success.

The Journey of Personal Growth

Personal growth is not a destination but a lifelong journey. As you develop new skills, overcome challenges, and expand your understanding of yourself and the world, you evolve constantly. The key to sustaining empowerment lies in your commitment to ongoing personal development. This commitment involves embracing change, seeking new learning opportunities, and staying open to self-improvement.

In this section, we will discuss how to keep the momentum of growth alive, ensuring that your progress continues to flourish. By cultivating a mindset of curiosity, resilience, and determination, you can continue growing in ways that support your long-term success. This ongoing journey of personal growth is about reaching new heights, deepening your connection with your true self, and living a life of purpose and authenticity.

The Importance of Lifelong Learning

Lifelong learning is the secret to sustained personal growth and empowerment. It's not enough to reach a certain level of knowledge or skill and stop; true empowerment comes from continually seeking new opportunities for learning and self-improvement. Continuous learning keeps your mind sharp, expands your horizons, and equips you with the tools to navigate an ever-changing world.

"Formal education will make you a living, self-education will make you a fortune."
— Jim Rohn

A mindset of curiosity and openness is essential for embracing lifelong learning. When you remain curious, you're more likely to explore new ideas, ask questions, and seek experiences that challenge your current understanding. This mindset keeps you engaged and motivated to grow, no matter where you are in life.

Education, both formal and informal, plays a significant role in lifelong learning. Whether through formal coursework, workshops, reading, or self-directed study, the pursuit of knowledge helps you stay relevant and adaptable in your personal and professional life. By continually expanding your knowledge and skills, you maintain the momentum of growth and ensure that your empowerment journey is ongoing.

Setting New Goals for Growth

As you continue on your journey of personal growth, it's essential to keep setting new goals that challenge and inspire you. Setting and pursuing new goals keeps you focused and driven, providing a clear direction for your ongoing development.

Techniques for setting new goals include reflecting on your current achievements and identifying areas where you want to grow even further. These goals should be specific, measurable, and aligned with your personal values and long-term vision. Regularly reassessing and adjusting your goals ensures they remain relevant and challenging, pushing you to reach new heights.

Celebrating milestones and acknowledging your progress is also crucial to stay motivated. Recognizing how far you've come helps reinforce your positive changes and encourages you to keep moving forward. By setting and achieving new goals, you continually build on your foundation of empowerment, creating a fulfilling and intentional life.

Change as a Catalyst for Growth

Change is an inevitable part of life, and how you respond to it can significantly impact your personal growth. Rather than fearing change, embracing it as a catalyst for development and empowerment is important. Change often brings with it new opportunities for learning, growth, and self-discovery, pushing you out of your comfort zone and into new areas of potential.

Staying adaptable and open to new opportunities is vital to thriving in the face of change. When you approach change with a positive and flexible mindset, you're more likely to see challenges as opportunities rather than obstacles. This adaptability allows you to confidently navigate life's transitions, using each experience as a stepping stone toward further growth.

Encouraging yourself to view challenges and changes as opportunities for further development is essential for sustaining empowerment. Every change, whether planned or unexpected, offers a chance to learn something new, gain new perspectives, and strengthen your resilience. By embracing change, you ensure that your journey of personal growth remains dynamic and fulfilling, continuously driving you toward greater empowerment and self-actualization.

The Power of Leading by Example

Leading by example is one of the most effective ways to inspire others to break free from the victim mentality. When people see the positive changes in your life—how you've transformed your mindset, overcome challenges, and taken control of your destiny—they are more likely to believe that they, too, can achieve similar results. Your personal transformation serves as a powerful testament to the possibilities of empowerment.

Authenticity and vulnerability are key when sharing your journey with others. Being honest about your struggles, setbacks, and successes makes your story relatable and genuine. Through this honesty, others can see that empowerment is not about perfection but about perseverance and growth. By sharing your experiences, you provide hope and a tangible example of what it looks like to overcome the victim mentality.

By embodying the principles of empowerment in your daily life, you create an environment where others feel inspired to pursue their own growth. Whether through casual conversations, mentoring, or simply living your values, your actions can motivate others to start their journey toward empowerment.

In our final chapter, we'll conclude our journey together and briefly recap some of the key lessons and themes throughout the book.

Chapter 12
A Few Final Thoughts

"By three methods we may learn wisdom: First, by reflection, which is noblest; Second, by imitation, which is easiest; and third by experience, which is the bitterest."

— Confucius

A S YOU REACH THE conclusion of this journey, it's important to pause and reflect on the progress you've made and the growth you've experienced. Empowerment is not just a destination—it's a continuous, evolving process that shapes every aspect of your life. Throughout this book, you've explored the tools, strategies, and mindset shifts needed to break free from the victim mentality and embrace a life of purpose, confidence, and self-ownership.

But this is just the beginning.

In this final chapter, we'll revisit the key lessons learned, celebrate the milestones achieved, and reinforce the importance of sustaining your journey. Empowerment is a powerful force, and by continuing to nurture it within yourself, you not only enhance your own life but also contribute to a larger movement of resilience, growth, and empowerment for others.

As you move forward, remember that this journey is uniquely yours. Embrace it with an open heart and a determined spirit, knowing that you have the tools and the power to shape your own destiny. Let this be a lifelong pursuit, filled with continuous learning, self-discovery, and the courage to keep growing, no matter what challenges come your way.

Reflecting on Your Progress and Growth

As you conclude this leg of your journey, it's essential to take a moment to recognize and celebrate the personal transformation you've undergone. Reflect on the key insights and growth you've achieved since embarking on this path. What began as a quest to overcome the victim mentality has now led you to the continuous journey toward an empowered mindset, characterized by confidence, resilience, and a sense of purpose.

As your journey continues, think about the milestones you've reached along the way—whether it's breaking free from self-defeating thoughts, setting and achieving meaningful goals, or establishing healthy boundaries in your relationships. These victories, no matter how small, are significant indicators of your progress and deserve acknowledgment. Celebrating milestones is not just recognizing past achievements; it's also strengthening the belief that you have the power to continue growing and evolving.

The Impact of Empowerment

Empowerment has a profound impact on your life. As you shift from a victim mentality to an empowered mindset, you'll notice positive changes in your relationships, career, and overall well-being. Empowerment enhances resilience, enabling you to navigate challenges with greater ease and confidence. It promotes a sense of fulfillment, as you begin to live in harmony with your values and aspirations.

Over time, periodically reflect on how these changes influence your day-to-day life. Perhaps you're becoming more assertive in your communication, more proactive in pursuing your goals, or more mindful of your emotional well-being. These shifts, driven by your newly empowered mindset, are contributing to a more balanced, fulfilling life. It's important to stress that these transformations don't happen overnight; they result from small, consistent efforts that, over time, lead to significant growth.

Take Note of the Lessons Learned

Every journey is filled with valuable lessons. In the days, weeks, and months to come, reflect on the key insights you've gained along the way. What challenges did you face, and how did you overcome them? What strategies proved most effective in helping you shift your mindset and sustain your progress? These lessons are important for your continued growth and serve as a source of wisdom that you can share with others.

The journey of empowerment is deeply personal and unique to each person. As you reflect on your own experiences, remember that the path to empowerment is not a straight line—it's a dynamic process involving successes and setbacks. The wisdom you've gained is invaluable, reinforcing the idea that empowerment is an ongoing process of self-discovery and growth.

As you move forward, carry these lessons with you, using them as a foundation for continued personal development. Remember that the insights and strengths you've gained serve as a guiding light on your path to a more fulfilling life.

Staying Resilient and Adaptable

Resilience is a crucial quality for sustaining empowerment over the long term. Life is full of unexpected challenges and uncertainties, and your ability to navigate these with strength and composure is a key indicator of your empowerment. Resilience allows you to bounce back from setbacks, learn from difficulties, and continue moving forward with determination.

Adaptability is equally important in your journey. As circumstances change, so too must your approach. Being adaptable means staying flexible in your thinking and behavior, allowing you to respond effectively to new situations and opportunities.

It involves being open to change, even when it's uncomfortable, and viewing these changes as opportunities for further growth.

Empowerment is not about rigidly sticking to one path but about being able to adjust your course as needed, always with an eye toward your long-term goals and values. By cultivating resilience and adaptability, you ensure that your journey of empowerment remains a central theme and you're responsive to whatever life brings your way.

Encouraging Others to Embrace Their Potential

Empowerment is a powerful force, not only in your own life but also in the lives of those around you. As you continue on your journey of personal growth and empowerment, you have a unique opportunity to inspire and uplift others. By sharing your experiences, offering support, and leading by example, you can encourage those around you to recognize and embrace their power and potential.

Helping others break free from the victim mentality and step into their full potential creates a ripple effect that can transform families, communities, and society. Empowerment isn't just about individual success; it's about contributing to a more significant movement of positive change. Whether through mentoring, offering guidance, or simply living your truth, you can profoundly impact those around you.

The Role of Empowerment in Inspiring Others

Personal empowerment is a transformative force in your life and can be used as a beacon of inspiration for those around you. When others see the changes you've made—how you've overcome challenges, developed resilience, and taken control of your life—they may feel motivated to pursue their own paths of growth and empowerment. Your journey can be a powerful example of what's possible, encouraging others to believe in their potential and take steps toward positive change.

Sharing your stories, insights, and experiences is vital to inspiring others. By openly discussing your journey—both the successes and the struggles—you provide a roadmap for those who may be facing similar challenges. Your authenticity and vulnerability can resonate with them, helping them see that empowerment is attainable for anyone willing to put in the effort.

This is not the End
It's Only the Beginning

As we conclude our journey together, it's important to take a moment to reflect on the progress you've made and the path that lies ahead. Empowerment is a lifelong pursuit that requires dedication, resilience, and an unwavering commitment to personal growth. Throughout this book, you've learned valuable tools and strategies to overcome the victim mentality, set empowering habits, and inspire others to embrace their potential. Now, as you continue forward, it's essential to carry these lessons with you and apply them in your daily life.

This is not the end, but rather a new beginning—an opportunity to continue growing, evolving, and creating the life you desire. Remember, the power to shape your future lies within you. By staying true to your values, setting meaningful goals, and embracing every challenge as an opportunity for growth, you will continue to thrive.

Let me remind you that you are capable, worthy, and empowered to live your best life. This journey of empowerment is yours to own, and with each step you take, you are creating a future filled with purpose, fulfillment, and endless possibilities.

With Love and Gratitude,

Donovan Garett

Where to Find Help

I F YOU (OR SOMEONE you care about) is in need of help, here is a list of agencies dedicated to providing free mental health support in the United States, Canada, the United Kingdom, and Mexico:

United States

National Suicide Prevention Lifeline: 24/7 free and confidential support for people in distress, prevention, and crisis resources.

- **Website**: suicidepreventionlifeline.org

- **Phone**: 1-800-273-TALK (8255) or 988 (crisis line)

SAMHSA's (Substance Abuse and Mental Health Services Administration) National Helpline: Free, confidential, 24/7 treatment referral and information service for individuals and families facing mental and/or substance use disorders.

- **Website**: samhsa.gov/find-help/national-helpline

- **Phone**: 1-800-662-HELP (4357)

Mental Health America (MHA): Advocacy, education, research, and support for mental health conditions; provides a range of resources and local support services.

- **Website**: mhanational.org

Crisis Text Line: Free, 24/7 text-based mental health support.

- **Website**: crisistextline.org

- **Text**: Text HOME to 741741

NAMI (National Alliance on Mental Illness)

1. **Services**: Free education, advocacy, and support groups for individuals with mental health conditions and their families.

2. **Website**: nami.org

Canada

Kids Help Phone: 24/7 free and confidential mental health support for young people in Canada.

- **Website**: kidshelpphone.ca

- **Phone**: 1-800-668-6868

- **Text**: Text CONNECT to 686868

Canadian Mental Health Association (CMHA): Mental health programs and services, public education, advocacy, and resources.

- **Website**: cmha.ca

Wellness Together Canada: Free mental health and substance use support, including one-on-one counseling.

- **Website**: https://wellnesstogether.ca/

- **Phone**: 1-866-585-0445

Crisis Services Canada: National network for suicide prevention and crisis intervention.

- **Website**: crisisservicescanada.ca / https://988.ca/

- **Phone**: 1-833-456-4566

- **Text**: Text 45645

- **Call or Text 9-8-8**

Indigenous Services Canada – Hope for Wellness Help Line: Immediate mental health counseling and crisis intervention to all Indigenous peoples across Canada.

- **Website**: hopeforwellness.ca

- **Phone**: 1-855-242-3310

United Kingdom

Samaritans: 24/7 free support for anyone in emotional distress or struggling to cope.

- **Website**: samaritans.org

- **Phone**: 116 123

Mind: Information, support, and advice for people experiencing mental health problems.

- **Website**: mind.org.uk

Rethink Mental Illness: Advocacy, support groups, and services for people affected by mental illness.

- **Website**: rethink.org

- **Phone**: 0300 5000 927

Shout: 24/7 text messaging service providing free mental health support.

- **Website**: giveusashout.org

- **Text**: Text SHOUT to 85258

The Mix: Free support and counseling for young people under 25.

- **Website**: themix.org.uk

- **Phone**: 0808 808 4994

Mexico

Línea de la Vida (National Mental Health Hotline): 24/7 mental health support and crisis intervention.

1. **Website**: gob.mx/salud

2. **Phone**: 800 911 2000

SAPTEL (Sistema de Atención Psicológica por Teléfono): Free psychological counseling via phone, available 24/7.

1. **Phone**: 55 5259 8121

Frente Nacional para la Sororidad: Support for women in abusive relationships and those experiencing psychological distress.

1. **Website**: frentenacional.mx

Centro de Integración Juvenil (CIJ): Mental health services focused on prevention and treatment of substance use disorders, including psychological counseling.

1. **Website**: https://www.gob.mx/salud/cij

2. **Phone**: 55 5212 1212

Mexican Red Cross – Psychological Support Services: Psychological support for individuals in crisis or affected by traumatic events.

1. **Website**: cruzrojamexicana.org.mx

2. **Phone**: 55 1084 9000

www.ingramcontent.com/pod-product-compliance
Lightning Source LLC
Chambersburg PA
CBHW030014290326
41934CB00005B/335